Happily Ever After

Faith Bleasdale

Cover photo by Thom Bleasdale

ISBN-13: 978-1482751543
ISBN-10: 1482751542

prologue

What does fantasy mean to me? It means a place I go to, to dream. It's a person I aspire to be. It's a life I yearn to live, or a situation that I am extending an invitation to. It means my hopes, my dreams my desires. Sometimes it means events that are unlikely to happen and others it means envisioning what I desperately want. Fantasy means a lot to me; I would be lost without it.

I believe everyone has fantasies. Some people have more than others; I certainly do. But we all dream, don't we? Who hasn't imagined the big house, the lottery win, the date with a supermodel or movie star, the fast car, the diamonds? Or maybe the less selfish among us dream of a world where there is no war, no hunger, no abuse and no fear. And there are people whose fantasies consist of what many of us take for granted; a hot meal, a roof over their head, being able to keep warm on a cold day, not feeling lonely. Dreams feed our souls and keep us alive; they make us who we are.

I believe that fantasies are a part of life and I am a fantasist. Not the type of fantasist who confuses fantasy and reality, trust me I know the difference, but I do have many, many fantasies. They inspire us; they motivate us they take us out of our normal day to day lives. They let us live in another world, a better world, a world we aspire to, rather than actually have.

Some may argue with me, there are people who never dream because they are happy with their lives. I probably wouldn't believe them but then if I did, I would say that people who never fantasise definitely lack ambition.

It's not always easy though. How many times do we say 'it wasn't supposed to be like this?' This wasn't what we imagined, or dreamed. That's reality. I am not saying that fantasy and reality can never be the same, but let's face it, it doesn't always happen. Especially if you aim high with your fantasies, which I certainly do. To me, life is a constant battle between fantasy and reality, or a constant shifting of fantasy to take reality into account. Does that make sense?

Because those battles, that shift, are a huge factor in my life. I have had to accept reality many times, when I would rather have my fantasy. I have had to accept reality when it is so awful; it's like my worst enemy. But what I won't do is lose my fantasies altogether, they are loyal friends to me. Reality fights fantasy and I am often the casualty of that war. But I will never give up on my dreams, and I will never stop searching for my Happily Ever After.

One : A Spinster of this Parish

I had always loved children and although I never wanted to work with them, I believed I would always be a mother one day. When I was much younger, when I was with my Ex and even now when I was alone, I imagined my future with children; I watched it as if it was a full colour feature film. I envisaged my babies and how my life would be. And, naturally it would be wonderful. I would be happily married to the man I loved (who would be like Prince Charming or George Clooney), I would have two, possibly even three gorgeous, clever children. I would be the perfect mother, and I would even have learnt to do more than boil an egg.

As our lives progressed in our dream home, I would be a successful career woman as well as a mother, my husband would share the chores, my children would flourish, be clever, talented and above all happy.

Honestly, we would be like a smaller more interesting and funny version of The Walton's.

I was technically single but Mr. Right was always just around the corner and after a whirlwind romance, and a wedding, (in Vegas naturally), I would conceive a honeymoon baby. I would have found my Prince Charming; we would have some little Charming's and we would all live happily ever after in our castle. Or at least in a nice flat.

In a London hospital I sat opposite gynaecology's answer to Creulla de Ville. She wasn't glamorous or wearing a fur coat, (I seem to recall she wore mainly beige), however she certainly looked as if she was

capable of killing puppies. She wordlessly examined me as I chattered nervously trying desperately to fill the ominous silence. Finally, we sat opposite each other.

'You don't have children,' she either said or asked. I couldn't be sure which.

'No,' I replied.

'You probably won't be able to have them,' she told me with a look on her face that suggested she ate children as well as killing puppies.

I barely remember the rest of the conversation. There was something about follow up appointments, maybe an operation. How as I only had one ovary, surgery would be a last resort but not to be ruled out at this stage. I vaguely remembered asking her if I would never have children, and she said, (rather gleefully I felt) that at this moment in time it looked unlikely. The room was filled with horrific white noise and I could no longer hear my voice. In between all this there were lots of words I didn't understand and certainly couldn't spell.

I thought back to that morning and tried to recapture how normal it felt. At the very least normal compared to now. As I got ready to go to the hospital I knew that I had something wrong with me but never in my wildest dreams did I imagine this. Optimistically I was convinced that it was nothing serious and a few pills would cure me. As I ate my breakfast (toast and marmite), as I got dressed (black jeans, Ugg boots and a black top), even as I anxiously made my way though the heavy London traffic, there wasn't even a tiny thought that this visit would ring the death knell of my fertility. If I had known that I never would have gone.

After being dismissed by the doc, I left the room in tears, where my friend was waiting.

'You were quick,' she said, but I felt as if I had been in that room forever.

I didn't tell her about the exchange, I blamed my tears on a horrible and invasive examination, which was true, but I didn't tell anyone their true cause. I played that visit over and over in my head trying to make sense of it as I shed tears full of fear, hurt and confusion.

I was at one with my fantasies; I believed in them. I might go as far as to say they were my best friends. I called it optimism. But optimism only stays around for so long. Like the commitment phobic lover it threatens to leave and you have to coax it to stay. But that took strength and at that stage, after everything I wasn't sure that I had that strength anymore. To say I felt sorry for myself was a huge understatement. I wrapped myself in sorrow, and I wore it like a cape.

I had never thought of myself as a victim but life had been less than kind to me the past few years. In fact I believed I had a sob story that any contestant on a TV singing show would covet.

TV Presenter: 'Introducing one of our older contestants, Faith Bleasdale.'

Faith (looks indignant at being called 'older'): 'Hi, I'm Faith and I don't want sympathy but I have had a bit of a tough time lately, really.'

TV Presenter (looks sympathetic): 'Why don't you tell us about it?'

Faith: 'Well my father passed away a couple of years ago. He and I were very close and I miss him every single day.' Faith wipes away a tear.

TV Presenter (head tilted): 'That's hard for you isn't it. Was he your musical inspiration?'

Faith: 'Yes, my childhood was filled with him singing and playing to me.'

TV Presenter: 'How sad but lovely. What happened next?'

Faith: 'Well then I moved to Singapore with my fiancé, and I had to deal with my grief as well as being in a new country away from family and friends.'

TV Presenter: 'But at least it was sunny, and you had your career and the love of a good man, right?'

Faith: 'Um, while there my career suffered a massive blow. I was at a very low point having lost my father and the job I loved.' Faith wipes away another tear.

TV presenter: 'But at least you had the man of your dreams.'

Faith: 'Yes I did, until he cheated on me then dumped me for some-one else and bought me a one way ticket back to England two years after me leaving everything for him.' Faith sobs for what feels like ages.

*TV Presenter (hands Faith a tissue and squeezes her shoulder):
'That's a sad story, what are you going to sing?'
Faith: 'I Will Survive, of course.'*
There was no way I could lose despite not being able to sing.

I might have failed miserably at not feeling sorry for myself but I felt as if I had lost a hell of a lot. Like a house I had been knocked down and all that remained were my foundations. It wasn't the worst thing that happened, but my relationship break-down was the culmination of a rough couple of years. Ten years of being with my ex disappeared in a puff of his cigarette smoke. I limped home, with a broken heart, a dislocated shoulder, (you should never try using a step ladder when you are angry or drunk or both, apparently), and an unsure, unstable future.

That's what happens with fantasy vs. reality; a battle I seemed fully embroiled in. I had imaged that I would be getting married but as I got off the plane into the cruel, cold English winter, that dream was over. As I started to dust myself off, my confidence was at an all time low, as was my self esteem. I believed him when he said he loved me, but it all seemed to have been a horrible sham. I could have literally spent the rest of my life spouting forth the bitter feelings and thoughts that followed the break-up, but that would bore all of us. Instead I had to try to get past the anger, banish thoughts of revenge, and my ex suffering in a most horrific way, (being boiled alive, or made to listen to *Agadoo* on a loop for the rest of his life, perhaps?), after all what good would that do anyone? No, on second thoughts, don't answer that. After all, I am only human.

The truth is that break-ups are terrible, and hurt is even worse, but you need to get back into life. Because even when your fantasies are cruelly taken from you, there is always another one waiting around the corner. Or there was for me, because reality might have left me with very little but fantasy never, ever would. You see, I choose my best friends well.

I might have a broken heart, or at least a slightly battered one, but that didn't mean it wouldn't heal. There was, apparently, someone for everyone and there would be someone out there for me. A gorgeous guy who was more deserving of me than my despicable ex, who turned out to be a dishonourable cad. No, I would meet a gentleman, a man of manners. And chivalrous, whereas my ex couldn't even spell that.

A year or so later, my chivalrous Prince Charming hadn't manifested himself. At the time of the visit to the gynaecologist I was in the midst of what I liked to think of as a 'flingette' with someone who didn't live near me. A travelling salesman, (actually something to do with computers but that didn't sound as exciting). But anyway, said man was only around for a certain amount of time I knew there was an expiration date. He would go home and we might exchange the odd email but then that would phase out and we would both move on. Deep down this was what I wanted. No one would hurt me like my ex did again. No one would get the chance. Damaged? Me? I was a whole china shop after the bull had finished.

It made me sad to admit this. I was a romantic at heart but disappointment had taken me over and cynicism had moved in with it. I kept telling myself that one day I would meet someone who would change all this and I would fall in love again. But I am not sure I ever believed myself. What I didn't want was to feel as hideous as I did the day I boarded the plane to London, not ever, ever again.

And my travelling salesman was not the man who was going to change this, despite the fact that we were having fun. When I got back from seeing Creulla de gynaecologist we went out for dinner. I painted a bright, red-lipsticked smile on my face and forgot what she said. I would grieve for being a mother at some stage but first I wanted a nice dinner and a whole lot of wine.

The next few days I thought about the diagnosis. I had an appointment with another specialist in two months time, and until that time I had to try to remain positive. It wasn't as if I had the ideal family environment to bring a child into at the time, not even close. But still I wondered if I would be able to cope with never being a mother. It seemed everything else that had been snatched from me could be replaced, even, eventually the dastardly ex. However, this couldn't. Could it? No matter how much I thought about it, none of it felt real and I wasn't sure how I would ever come to terms with it. Or even if I would ever come to terms with it. And yet another very dark place beckoned.

I took the only step that I could in my quest for self-survival. I entered into a place I knew well; denial. I had been in denial about my ex for ages, because I couldn't confront the reality. So, I was a seasoned traveler to denial, I had a free pass; I even knew the way without a map. So off I went again.

Because the alternative, confronting the truth, was far too scary. My future looked more than grim. I would be a spinster of my parish. I was barren. And I didn't even like cats that much.

Denial was my safety net. And I needed it to catch me yet again.

So, I mentally listed what was good in my life; my family, my friends, my health (well apart from the ovary thing), my writing, my shoes, nice-ish hair... It wasn't the worst list, but then it wasn't the best either.

Motherhood is something most of us take for granted until 'for granted' takes it away.

Two : A brief dating history of Miss Faith Elizabeth Bleasdale

Fabulous thirty-something woman seeks man, 34-40, tall, well quite tall but not too tall (between 5ft9 and 6ft2). Own yacht and teeth. GOSH essential, hair optional, private jet a bonus, for non- superficial relationship.

At the time of the gynaecologist visit, I had been single for about a year. After ten years with the same man I was single, in my thirties and forget for a minute the broken heart, the thing that terrified me the most wasn't that I was on my own, it was the idea of dating again. I couldn't remember the last time I had a date, let alone what I wore to said date. I last dated in the days before everyone had mobile phones. I used to wait for the landline to ring. Oh my goodness, I last dated before texting was invented. Were the dinosaurs even extinct then?

I didn't want to date, that much I knew, but I still wanted the fantasy. I wanted love, I wanted marriage and I wanted children. And since I was now single the only way for me to get any of the above was for me to get back on the horse, (although not literally of course); I would have to date. In the absence of arranged marriages I had no choice.

I had no idea how dating worked in my post break-up world. My single friends weren't much help; they just told me horror stories about how guys still didn't call. Or more accurately most guys didn't call text or email. It seemed the more ways of communicating that had become available just gave men more means by which to ignore you. But if you were lucky enough to have a relationship they would break up by text or email rather than telling you to your face or calling. No one knew the rules because apparently there were no rules. Just a whole sea of sharks out there ready to eat you up and spit you out. It should have been enough to send me running to the nunnery.

Instead I decided to throw myself to said sharks and try to meet my Mr. Right. Because somewhere deep down I still believed in him. I might have been wearing disappointment but soon the summer collections would be out and I would be ready for a whole new wardrobe. Modern dating might be as confusing as trying to put flat pack furniture together when the instructions were in Japanese but hey, I would master it. Wouldn't I?

I decided to discover what the dating industry had to offer. I tried not to think about the fact that BE (before ex) there wasn't really a dating industry, just those leaflets they put through the door about matchmaking services which always had pictures of people with bad hair on them.

Anyway, I started with the obvious: internet dating.

Internet dating was genius. There was a whole website or number of websites full of guys who wanted to date you, (or me). Negotiating those sites was like being in a giant shopping mall. I was shopping for a man and one thing I was good at was shopping. All I needed was a photo, a profile and hundreds of guys would get in touch with me. I put up a photo, and admittedly in it I looked slightly drunk, or a bit of a psycho, or both actually, and I filled in my profile which according to my friends made me sound mean. But at least it matched the bad photos. I then waited. And waited. No one contacted me. And it cost me a fortune to be ignored because I subscribed for two months by accident. But I did learn a valuable lesson; rejection from strangers is almost as bad as rejection from people you know. Oh and when you think your self-esteem can't get any lower; it can.

When later I was persuaded back to internet dating I did actually have two dates. One guy was about five stone heavier than in his picture and had lost all his hair. The problem with that was that although he had misled me by putting a photo up of him from about ten years previous, I was the one who felt shallow for leaving as quickly as possible without being rude and refusing a second date. The second guy looked as he did in his photo but had a chip on his shoulder and was verging on the aggressive with everything he said. It was quite a stressful date, as he picked at everything I said, making me want to be mute. After that I broke up with internet dating, and it was my easiest break-up ever.

Not one to be defeated, I tried speed dating. This, I knew, would be better because there were real men in a room and I would get to speak to them, and perhaps not look as if I should be sectioned. A friend came with me for moral support and we got three minutes to talk to each guy before a really annoying bell would ring and the guys would move on. Whereas all the other girls took it seriously, my friend and I drank too much and I couldn't remember any men past about number ten. To make matters worse I did kiss number twenty-two, the last guy, and I didn't even remember that. I also gave him my phone number and he used it (by texting) and I did go on a date with him, although (and I am not proud of this, trust me), I had no memory of him at all. To cut a very sad story short, he had crazy hair, was wearing an anorak and terrible shoes. He then became my text pest; he texted me for a year afterwards before giving up. I have to admit, thinking about it, that I miss him a little bit. But that wasn't the point, the point was that dating or trying to date should carry health warnings. I was literally on a crash course of modern dating. And I wasn't very good at it.

I went to a supper club, I went to a 'lock and key' party, I went on a blind date, I even went zoo dating, (a singles day at London Zoo, and yes it was as bizarre as it sounds). It was entertaining but I didn't meet anyone apart from an ageing Elvis look-a-like who didn't look anything like Elvis and the less said about him the better. I tried just normal nights out, but that didn't produce Mr. Right either. I went on a lunch date with a guy who took me to a charity shop afterwards and tried to buy a fax machine. I even met a guy who I was convinced was gay, but wasn't and not only did he turn out to be straight but he also turned out to be married.

In the days before my ex, I met guys the old fashioned way. Either through friends or on an evening out, but that didn't seem to work anymore. My friends didn't know any single guys and if they did they would have been dating them themselves. I met men, I dated men, I texted men, I sometimes got texted back. It was all quite exhausting, it certainly kept my mind of my ex, but it didn't exactly seem to be heralding my future.

I always believed that love didn't happen if you looked for it, and you should leave it to fate. So I wasn't sure why I was not only looking, but also spending good money on it. There was something very wrong with the picture. It wasn't me and even if I was in a bad place at that time, it never would be. I was looking for something, too hard, as if love and I were playing a game of hide and seek, but love was a much better hider than I was seeker. The problem was that I had no idea how to stop.

I announced I would stay in, and if by any slim chance I met someone he would probably be a postman or a tradesman, but my friends told me in this day and age going out was essential, in order not to end up alone. And I began to wonder if ending up alone was that bad after all.

Because I dated. I dated tall men, short men, young men and old men (actually not that old). I dated a guy whose idea of a cocktail was vodka and Redbull. I dated a guy who lied about his age, and said that although he was fifty he looked as if he was in his mid-thirties, which he didn't. I dated a guy who did have a yacht (or at least a boat) but wore a football strip despite not being a footballer. It was raining men and I needed a new umbrella.

I was barely getting to a third date, let alone anything else. With my ex I saw a future with him quite soon into the relationship but since him I hadn't met a guy who I could see myself being with. Of course perhaps I wasn't ready, because deep down I knew it was my fault; I was attracting guys that I didn't actually like, or that I had nothing in common with or who didn't like me; actually I was attracting guys who there was no threat of me falling in love with or who would never fall in love with me. And to fully ensure that this didn't happen I would sabotage every date with anyone of promise. Boy, I was good. I was writing a dating column and seemed intent on turning myself into a more hopeless version of Bridget Jones. Actually I managed to make Bridget Jones look like a dating guru. A therapist would have had a field day with me. Actually thinking about it, I could have kept a whole pack of therapists busy for years.

I believe love and fate are intrinsically linked but perhaps since the advent of internet dating, fate has decided to take a well earned holiday.

Three : The Thin Blue Lines

When I lived in Singapore I heard about a woman who had adopted a Chinese baby girl. A bit Angelina Jolie. But why not? Although I didn't have her looks, her money, her career or Brad Pitt, I could do it. I might not be able to have a baby but I could adopt. If not in my own country then somewhere there would be a baby who needed a mummy. After all I was a would-be mummy who needed a baby.

Grief was someone I was familiar with; it had kind of become a flatmate of sorts. I had and was still grieving for my father; I was also grieving for my relationship and my old life. I, at some point, would grieve for the child I thought I would never have. I was grieving for the fantasies that had deserted me. Although grief is horrible and about letting go, it is also about finding a way to face the future. I would never 'get over' my Dad's death but I had to learn to live without him. I missed the work I did but I knew I would have a great future career. I would never fully accept the way my ex treated me but I would have a future without him. I might not give birth to a child but I would find away to have one if that was what I wanted to do. That's how we continue with life. Whenever we are dealt a blow we take it. We may fall down but we then get up again. That's the remarkable thing about the human spirit. It finds a way of surviving.

Just over two months after my consultation with Cruella De Gynaecologist, I was standing in the ladies loo in *McDonalds* in Hampstead staring at a test that told me I was pregnant. Before you think I am a regular frequenter of McDonalds, I am not, I only go there as a special treat.

I was in *Boots*, with my friend, and *McDonalds* happened to be next door.

'Faith, we need to get this test done,' my friend pushed.

'Don't want to,' I replied like a sulky child. 'I want a Happy Meal.'

'I'll buy you one if you take the test.' You get the idea.

Obediently and trying not to think about my less than ostentatious surroundings I locked myself in the loo cubicle. The little blue lines appeared straight away. I didn't even have to wait thirty seconds let alone the two minutes it said on the box. I held the stick in one hand and the instructions in the other as I compared the picture of the positive result on the paper to that on my stick. I had to concede they were identical. Unsure what to do with the pee ridden stick; I shoved it back in the box and into my handbag.

When I walked out to find my Happy Meal waiting on the table I could only think that I was already a bad mother.

Because of the fact that I couldn't be pregnant it hadn't occurred to me for one second that I was. Well it wouldn't would it? My periods hadn't been regular for a while; I'd been ill and on antibiotics for a throat infection, so I didn't feel great anyway; I was drinking copious amounts of water; I was peeing for the UK; my boobs had been tender for ages; I just started throwing up; I was exhausted. Finally if those glaring signs weren't enough I had completely gone off wine, (which trust me was perhaps the most alarming of all).

The friend who had taken me to *Boots* and *McDonalds* had been suggesting to me for a while that I was pregnant. I told her it was impossible. Because as far as I was aware it was. I saw a doctor because I thought I might be diabetic. I wasn't. No one apart from my friend thought I was pregnant. I only agreed to do the test to shut her up. In actual fact, it shut us all up pretty quickly.

As I ate my 'Happy Meal,' I had suddenly, overnight, become a candidate for *The Jeremy Kyle Show*. Only with much better hair. Imagine single mother-to-be takes her pregnancy test in the loo at *McDonalds*.

I suppose at least my baby wasn't conceived there.

But I couldn't think about that as I had too much else to figure out. Not least how I managed to spend so much on bloody pregnancy tests.

The *McDonalds* test wasn't my first. Oh no. That morning, (on my friend's orders) I went and bought two pregnancy tests in order to prove once and for all that there was no way I was with child. I chose the idiot proof digital ones that spelt out (literally) if you're pregnant or not. The emotions that were running through me at this time were pretty horrific to deal with. When it was first suggested I might be pregnant, I wanted to shout and scream and say, no, that was the cruellest part because I couldn't be. Then I thought my body was playing a horrible trick on me. But I was feeling so physically bad that mentally I had little strength to fight the bad taste joke that was going on. Because there was a tiny part of me that wondered if I was. And then, if I was how could that be? And then if that could be, what would I do?

The first test definitely didn't say 'pregnant' or 'not pregnant'. As I studied the idiot-proof instructions, it had an error message. I drank half a litre of water and did the second test. It had the same result. How on earth can you do a pregnancy test wrong? Did I pee too much? Not enough? Did I hold the stick at the wrong angle? How can a fool-proof pregnancy test be so complicated? How could I be so stupid? Really, did they let people become mothers who couldn't even make the bloody test work?

So I went back to the chemist (the young man behind the counter must have thought I was neurotic and he gave me a sympathetic look, the kind of look that made me feel special but not in a good way), and got another, different make of high-tech test. This time I was determined to get my answer. Only this one came up with an error as well. I can honestly say I'd rarely felt more stupid and I wanted to give up, figuring that the tests not working was a sign that I wasn't pregnant; but when I told my friend what happened she was unrelenting.

So, over thirty pounds later I went and got the cheapest most basic pack of two tests and that was how I ended up in *McDonalds'* with a positive result.

I would love to say that I was filled with a rush of thoughts and emotions as I glanced at the pee covered stick, but I can't remember thinking anything much of note, apart from how undignified it was and how I needed to scrub my hands, oh and of course how I needed the burger more than ever. Perhaps I was in shock, but more likely I knew that there was so much I needed to think about that I decided not to think about anything. Remember how good I was at denial? I wasn't about to stop now. My friend was very excited, and although surprised at first she was soon celebrating on my behalf. I was just a little bit numb, very nauseous and tired, a tiredness I had never experienced before. Like a dysfunctional sleeping beauty I felt I could sleep for a hundred years.

But before I could do that, I had to tell my mother.

My mum's lovely and we were very close. But she's also fairly old-fashioned and well, I didn't discuss my love life (or whatever it should be called) with her. Ever. So when she answered the phone, I asked her if she was sitting down.

'Yes,' she replied sounding a bit puzzled.

'Well, mum I seem to be a bit pregnant.' Nice and to the point. There was a silence.

'Oh,' she said eventually. 'I didn't know you were seeing anyone.'

'Well, I'm not anymore. But well, you know.' I wondered for a minute if she would believe it was an immaculate conception. But as naïve as my mum was, even she wouldn't buy that I was the chosen one, or even that God had got the wrong house by mistake.

'Right. Well, gosh. When is the baby due?'

'I don't know; I don't know anything right now, but I think it's good.' I felt about five years old, not because my mum was cross but because I knew that this wasn't news anyone, (including me) was expecting to hear.

I talked to her a bit more, told her not to tell anyone, and then I said goodbye.

'Is it too early for a drink?' she asked.

'Mum it's three in the afternoon.'

'Great, well I might just go and get the sherry.'

Not only was I a bad mother to be, but now I was a bad daughter who had driven her mother to drink.

I felt it only fair to call my brother, just in case my mother needed picking up off the floor or something. I begged him not to be cross before I said anything, and I think he might have thought I had gambled his inheritance away or sold our mother into a cult so he was actually a bit relieved when I told him. In fact, he reacted a bit like if I'd told him that I had changed my brand of shampoo. But I knew he was secretly excited.

'You better go and earn some money,' he said, helpfully.

'Yes, I know.'

'Because you can't come and live with me.' Oh yes, he was really excited.

I am doing my family a disservice, because they were understandably a bit shocked by my news. My mother, (when she sobered up) was actually immediately incredibly excited about becoming a grandma and she even said she needed to change her car – I lived a five hour drive from her – and then questioned me about what I was eating. My brother said that he would teach the child to surf and skateboard, which was very helpful seeing as it was probably the size of a grain of rice.

I called my flatmate who was really shocked, and I told my friend's mother (as I was staying with them), who was also shocked. Even I was shocked. We were like a whole tribe of shocked people. At this stage I didn't want to tell anyone else. I toyed, briefly with the idea of calling Creulla but then I didn't have her number, or even her real name. I even did one last pregnancy test when I got home to check, which was also positive. So, it was time for me to leave Denial. I just hoped I knew the way.

Motherhood begins when the blue lines appear.

Four: The caring profession?

I was pregnant. I was single but that didn't matter because I would have the support and love of my family and friends. And my baby would be loved, and nurtured and adored. And perhaps one day there would be a guy who would make a wonderful father to my child, but if not then I would be mother and father. I would be the best parents ever. Oh and I would be beautiful and thin and rich.

My fling had well and truly flung. I was single and pregnant. I barely remember how I reacted; I certainly didn't know how I actually felt. Too many emotions were sprinting around my head, and I couldn't catch any of them. My best friend was 'super' excited, my mother turned to sherry and my brother acted as if I told him I had decided to have pasta for dinner. And me, well I gave up drinking and Happy Meals.

Emotionally reality hadn't sunk in, but practically it had. My instinct kicked in and whatever else was going on I had to protect what was growing inside me. I booked an appointment with my doctor. But apart from that I didn't really know much about being pregnant. At that moment all I could concentrate on was being sick and feeling tired. I had moments of intense panic but at that stage instead of exploring their origins I pushed them away, I knew I would have to think about the future and the reality but for now all I could do was to try to put one foot in front of the other, and keep panic at arm's length.

Two days later I walked into my doctor's surgery. I saw a female doctor who I'd never met before and who reminded me of my school hockey teacher (butch, mean, looked terrible in a skirt).

'What can we do for you?' she asked, which annoyed me because there was only one of her and she didn't seem to be even a tiny bit royal.

'I did a pregnancy test and it said I was pregnant but I have this ovary thing and I can't get pregnant.'

'Um, I see from your notes. But you are?'

'Yes.'

'Are you happy?' she asked, in a way which suggested she wasn't.

'Well it wasn't planned, because of the ovary thing,' I replied.

'Yes but are you happy?' Her manner was a bit abrasive. In fact, she was the *Brillopad* of doctors. I nodded being too scared to speak.

She asked me about my last period. I hazarded an educated guess, having never been very good with numbers.

'Well it's early days, I wouldn't go buying the school uniform yet.' I blinked in case I was hearing things.

'Right.'

'Anyway, I'll get you the midwife's number.' She left me sitting there still wondering if I was allowed to be a bit offended. She came back, gave me a number on a yellow post-it note and told me to call them.

'Right.' I said, again.

'I'm sure you expected whistles and bells but we don't do that.'

I slunk out of her room feeling that the headmistress had just dismissed me after a telling off. As I walked home the wind taunted me and the rain suddenly joined in, it hit me that this was about as far from how I had imagined things as was possible.

Perhaps I had expected whistles and bells, or perhaps just a bit of warmth and kindness. I knew it was early days and there were risks, which is why I'd kept the news fairly quiet, but also I didn't think worrying about that was going to do me any good. I thought she could have been a bit nicer and also talked to me about the process. I told her this was my first baby, but she was unmoved. I wonder if I had told her that

I was a single pregnant woman she might have lined me up and shot me. Instead, she just said I needed to see the Midwife and that was it.

I had a mental list of things to ask her, from what I should be eating to what I should be taking, but her manner rendered me incapable of asking anything.

Instead I went to my chemist on the way home who told me to immediately take folic acid, and gave me some advice on how to deal with my other symptoms. Why the hell couldn't the doctor have done that? Perhaps she really was a hockey teacher masquerading as a doctor. And perhaps insanity was yet another of my pregnancy symptoms.

I called my mother (who by now was incredibly sober and talking about prams), and she said she was going to complain to her MP about my doctor. And then I went and ate some sweets. They made me feel much better until ten minutes after I'd finished them when I was sick.

My continued anger with the doctor was being used to distract me from other things. Like reality. Because it was real now. I was pregnant; I had to see a midwife. And I had never seen one of those before. I had a baby inside me and although I didn't know much, I knew that. I didn't know how I felt, it all happened to so quickly. It was as if life was playing in fast forward. In the space of a couple of months I had gone from being told I couldn't have children to being pregnant. And now I had to think about what next, because if I was going to do this I would have to do it alone.

Growing a life inside felt somehow like one of the most important, special things I had ever done. I might not be the ideal candidate to be a mother (after all I was a bit of a party girl, and a terrible cook and half the time unable to look after myself properly let alone anyone else), but I knew that my child would be loved by me and my family. I knew that the baby would be nourished, and cherished and never abused or left hungry. I knew that I might not be in the best situation but I was certainly not in the worst. I knew that I was very lucky but I could also say that in many ways the baby would be lucky too.

What followed was an inner struggle. I would go from feeling euphoric to thinking, or knowing, that I couldn't do it and I couldn't do it alone.

There was a lot of soul searching, conflict, reality and fantasy changing yet again. In the end, there was little choice. I thought that I couldn't have the baby and I couldn't not have the baby. Try and reconcile that.

A voice deep down said the events that led me to where I found myself were telling me that this baby was meant to be and who was I to argue with that? Fate had been playing its cards up until now, so perhaps I should continue to let it finish the game. I just hoped that fate knew what it was doing. Because I sure as hell didn't.

The horrid doctor made me think. I went to her having not really thought about the baby any more than I had to, and I came away thinking about nothing else. I came away wondering if I was doing the wrong thing. I came away wondering if I even could do it. But I knew that I wasn't and I could. In my heart, despite the huge hill I was about to climb and the obstacles that might be lying in wait, I knew that it was going to be OK. More than OK, it was going to be wonderful.

Pregnancy should be about bells and whistles

Five: The first trimester

'Up next is the brilliant and quite frankly inspirational Faith Bleasdale. As all of you who haven't been in Outer Mongolia for the last few months will know, Faith has written an international bestselling book, "How to be good at being pregnant". As a result women everywhere are forever in her debt. Because there is no doubt that Faith Bleasdale is the best at being pregnant ever. So, it is my great pleasure to bring out the beautiful Faith.' Huge round of applause and cheers in the studio as I made my way to the sofa.

I wasn't very good at pregnancy. I already had a number of symptoms before I discovered I was pregnant, but now they seemed to be growing by the minute. Joining the sore boobs, (they felt as if they'd been repeatedly attacked by a sledgehammer) the tiredness and the nausea were constant headaches, constant trips to the loo and a constant horrible taste in my mouth. How on earth did women hold down a normal job when they were pregnant? I couldn't even hold down my abnormal one.

The weird taste in my mouth might have been metallic although I can't be sure as I didn't normally eat metal. It was horribly unpleasant and the only way to combat it was to suck mints, but after a while I actually hated the taste of them too.

My boobs were never exactly tiny, but suddenly they were almost rivalling those of an enhanced glamour model. It was as if someone had taken a bicycle pump and inflated them overnight and my favourite dress which was normally very chaste made me look as if I was advertising my wares. And my wares suddenly took me, let alone any innocent bystander, by surprise. I relegated said dress to the back of the wardrobe and spent a small fortune on new bras. I also had to give up sleeping on my front. Actually I'm not sure I ever did sleep on my front but I definitely no longer had that option. I was terrified that they would keep growing until I would no longer be able to stand up without falling over. You may laugh but my fears were very real.

I was also trying not to give in to my tiredness but as soon as I hit my pillow I would be asleep. I didn't actually need a pillow; one afternoon I was sitting on the sofa staring at my laptop and the next thing I knew I was waking up. The worst thing was that without being able to tell people why I was so tired, I found that I would yawn when in meetings or with friends, giving the impression that I was either incredibly bored or leading an exciting life. Some of the time the former was the case but the latter certainly wasn't. I decided the best thing would be not leaving the house, which was easier said that done.

I told my flatmate that I was so tired it hurt.

'But you're always moaning about being tired,' she said.

'OK fair point but it's never been like this before.'

'Christ, it must be bad.' Then I realised that I always moaned about feeling tired and now I felt a bit like the girl who cried wolf, so if I needed sympathy I had to talk about other symptoms.

Luckily I had enough of them to choose from.

A lot of people have said that morning sickness is an inappropriate name, and totally misleading. I had morning, lunchtime and afternoon sickness. The only meal I could keep down was dinner and that was only if I ate after seven. My relationship with my loo bowl was more intimate than either of us would have liked, and the constant vomiting was really nasty; the only good thing I could think was that I would never become bulimic. Looking on the bright side isn't as easy as you think sometimes.

I don't want to harp on about sickness, too much, because it's such a horrible topic and it is what it is, but I will say that even when I wasn't throwing up I felt nausea sitting in me, like a threatening squatter. So my lovely mother sent me some of those acupressure wrist bands that you get for travel sickness. I wore one on each wrist and they worked sometimes, but not always. However I was grateful that they at least did something. I tried eating ginger biscuits too, but I think I went too far because the packet was suddenly empty and I felt really sick again.

The annoying thing was that I was eating healthily most of the time. Because after I was sick I was hungry, and it seemed in the midst of a vicious circle. Eat, be sick, eat etc. And the only time I didn't feel nauseas was when I was actually eating. So I was going to all the trouble of making salads, cooking home made dishes, (which for someone who can't cook was no mean feat). Occasionally I would succumb to a shop bought pizza or sandwiches but on the whole I was trying to be healthy for my baby. I would have fresh fruit for breakfast and salad or vegetables with every meal. I even went so far as to make my own vegetable juice (I was a star pupil when it came to my five a day). I would peel carrots, chop celery, add beetroot, cucumber, ginger and mint. I would put them through my juicer, which I would meticulously clean afterwards. And after drinking my delicious (yeah right), healthy, time consuming juice I more often than not threw it all up. I might as well have eaten crisps constantly.

My final and worst symptom was the headaches. I didn't normally suffer from headaches, (finally something I could moan about which I didn't normally, yay!) But most days I woke up with a headache, carried it round with me all day and went to sleep with said headache and if I remembered being asleep it might have been with me then. I read that pregnancy headaches were quite common so I wasn't unduly worried but I was in pain. I wondered if the fact I'd given up caffeine, alcohol and was being so sick meant it must have been some kind of detox effect. Whatever I just wanted them to go away.

The nurse at my surgery (no way was I risking the mean doctor), said I could take *Paracetemol* but I was neurotic, so I didn't want to do that. Instead I called my mummy.

My mother spoke to her pharmacist who she seemed to have on speed dial (he suggested the wristbands), and she sent me packets of cooling strips that you stick to your head which relieve the pain. And they worked. Oh it was so nice to have relief from the constant pounding pain. Drug free and effective, I was a total convert. They quickly became my favourite accessory.

Luckily I didn't go out much. Because not only was my stomach getting bigger, (which as I was so sick I didn't understand), but I was wearing wrist bands and a cooling strip on my head. Goodness, I looked like a pregnant Bjorn Borg.

I couldn't help but think that it was probably a good job I was single.

It's true, pregnancy is amazing, it's also totally baffling.

Six: It's a sacrifice

Giving up men was easy, after all the only guys who would be interested in a pregnant woman would be either the father of the child or plain weird. Giving up drinking and smoking was easy because I was going to be a mother and all that mattered was the health of my child. I would glow with health and everywhere I went people would say how much pregnancy suited me. If I was going to do this alone I was going to do it in style.

Reality was creeping closer and closer, and going to my first mid-wife's appointment was the next step. And I would be lying if I said I wasn't absolutely terrified; after Cruella and the mean doctor I didn't really hold out much hope for a warm reception.

I wondered why a midwife was called a midwife, so I googled it. The best answer was that the name was given to a woman hundreds of years ago who would be 'with the wife' when she gave birth. I wondered if mine should be renamed 'midsinglegirl,' (not quite the same ring; but I was in the midst of pregnancy madness after all), but actually I was quite pleased that in this politically correct mad country that the title hadn't been messed with. It was amazing how managing to distract myself with that stopped me thinking about the impending visit.

Luckily I needn't have worried. The midwife, S, was so lovely that from the word go I felt at ease. Even when she presented me with forms to fill in and tests to face, and stuff to read she didn't manage to scare me. She also booked my first scan, which I looked to as the milestone after which I would definitely be able to celebrate my pregnancy. I was also definitely cheered up by the fact that I got free dental care, because I hadn't been to the dentist for years due to the crippling cost. Although I don't think it's good to say that the best thing about pregnancy was free dentistry, but when you're being sick three times a day it is definitely an upside.

I felt able to talk to S about my symptoms and she gently reassured me. She gave me numbers so if I was ever worried I could always call someone. I hoped that I wouldn't end up being panicked by everything and calling them constantly, like a midwife phone stalker, but then I couldn't really be sure.

She was also supportive when I said I was going to be doing it alone. Instead of being judgmental (deep down I expected everyone to judge me), she made me feel that I was doing something great, and I was; I was going to have a baby.

I knew I was pregnant from the test, but that didn't mean I really *knew*. I had accepted it, adapted my lifestyle accordingly, but it's hard to explain, there was an element of unreality about it all. It still hadn't sunk in properly, or completely. I might be getting a bit bigger, and have enough physical symptoms to convince myself that I was carrying a baby but that didn't mean that I really understood it. I hated to sound even more insane but it was a big, no a huge, thing to get your head around.

But as I left the lovely midwife, clutching my folder it was definitely seeping in a bit more. I had also now got a book, sort of an 'everything you need to know about pregnancy', and although I accidentally looked at some horrific pages showing a woman giving birth, I was determined to read it, and ensure that I knew what I was doing for the sake of my unborn child. I was also determined not to look at the labour pictures, not even when I was going to have to do it myself. They say ignorance is bliss and when it came to that I was inclined to agree. Because what I saw made me want to cross my legs forever.

Instead I read about what I needed to do to ensure that I took proper care during my pregnancy. I would be good at being pregnant, if it was the last thing I did. So, I read what I needed to do in order to ensure gave my unborn child the best possible start.

<u>Some of the things I had given up:</u>
Alcohol (not a drop had passed my lips)
Prawns, oysters and Sushi
Camenbert, brie and stilton
Paté
Parma ham or any raw or undercooked meat
Swordfish
Caffeine (coffee and fizzy drinks)
Hair dye
Excessive exercise
Dating (my own addition that didn't apply to most pregnant women).

I was also avoiding liver but I never ate it anyway so can't claim that as a sacrifice. And excessive exercise wasn't something I regularly did to be honest. And I can't remember the last time I had swordfish. Let's face it, my dating history had been pretty grim so I'm not sure how much of a sacrifice that was either.

Although realistically I knew it would be probably at least the very least a year before I had another date, so it was a shame that the last one was so terrible. If I'd known it was going to be my last for the fore-seeable future I might have made sure it was enjoyable, (although how I would have done that I have no idea). But given my recent dates, I really don't think that was really like having to give something up; more like being saved from it to be honest.

My flatmate said that I wasn't necessarily going to have to give up men.

'Don't be silly, I'm pregnant and I am starting to resemble a whale,' I said. Not that I wanted to date, by the way.

'But there are men out there who really go for pregnant women,' she protested.

'You mean perverts?'

'Well yes.'

'Great.'

'Some men pay good money. It's just a thought. Prams are really expensive after all.'

There is a classic love story that someone told me about where the heroine discovered she was pregnant after her relationship broke down. When she was clearly showing she met a handsome young man who wooed her. Unable to believe her luck she tried to resist but found herself falling in love with him. They got together despite her pregnancy and lived happily ever after.

I later discovered that this was a *Neighbours* storyline.

The good thing about the amount of information available for pregnant women was that we could do more to ensure that the baby would be healthy, and we also knew what was happening to us which in theory meant we didn't panic. The bad thing about it was that there was such a thing as too much information, which could lead to confusion which could then lead to an overactive imagination; especially if you had one of those already. It could also actively encourage neurosis.

There seemed to be so much that you shouldn't do, eat, think etc. And if you looked at various websites you might be met with conflicting views. Drink, don't drink; eat this, don't eat this; exercise, don't exercise. What was a girl to think?

My mother said that when she had us there wasn't half as much advice out there as there is now and she just got on with it. I was grateful for the information and I did abide by it (like teacher's pet really), but I also found it overwhelming at times. One thing I read started lecturing about putting on too much weight. Although I can see why you don't want to be the size of a house, pregnancy wasn't really a good time to become neurotic about your weight. When you are faced with the hormonal challenges, feeling ill, tired, and emotional all which contributed to feeling vulnerable, did you really want to be told; 'don't eat that or you'll get really fat and you'll never get your shape back,'? I didn't think so. On the list of foods to avoid this book had added chocolate, biscuits, cakes and sweets. Well I tell you what I did with that book; I put it in the dustbin and went and got myself a bar of chocolate.

I did agree with not eating for two, which was a myth that unfortunately for us was exploded a while back. Yes, your baby needs a balanced diet and lots of vegetables and blah, blah, blah, but your baby also really needs a sane mother, not one who is a dribbling wreck because she really wants a *Snickers* but has been told she can't have one. I sometimes wondered who wrote these books, and had a sneaking suspicion that the authors were secretly men.

But I was being good. I filled in all my forms; I was taking folic acid every day; I swam three times a week and had ordered a yoga DVD for when I was over the three month mark. Although I was very tired, I was even going to stop napping most of the day away. Gosh, if they gave medals for being pregnant, perhaps I should have got one after all. Yes I was still ill and donning my Bjorn Bjorg look, (I went to *Tesco* and forgot I was wearing my head strip and couldn't understand why people were staring), but I felt reality nibbling away at me like a little squirrel with a nut.

I was now refusing to give into my mounting excitement because I hadn't got to my first scan yet, not because of anything else; not because of denial but because of fear. Now I was afraid that I would lose my baby, which meant that not only had I accepted it but I loved it; because you can only lose something that you feel you have already got.

A mum- to- be puts her unborn child's needs first, because in her heart she is already a mum.

Seven: Enormous knickers

One of the most popular chapters from my best selling book, 'How To Be Good at Being Pregnant', is the chapter on how I remained beautifully slim throughout my pregnancy. Of course I had a healthy baby bump but it was incredibly neat and I didn't put weight on anywhere else. Read the book if you want to find out the secret to my incredible success.

I couldn't understand how I was being sick several times a day yet still putting on weight. My stomach was expanding and although I was still kidding myself I could fit into my skinny jeans, in reality, I could barely get the button done up. It made no sense and no matter how hard I tried to figure it out I couldn't. I dived into my 'Everything you need to know about pregnancy and lots of stuff you don't' book and I called my friend in a panic.

'I'm having twins,' I told my friend.

'Oh shit, did you have a scan already?'

'No, I just know I am, my book says that all my symptoms and my size strongly suggests it.'

'Are you mad?' Of course I wasn't mad as I explained how I had ticked all the expecting twins boxes. I was very sick, I was bigger than most people are when they're just a bit pregnant (I looked as if I had a regular beer drinking habit), and there was a history of twins in my family, (my fraternal grandmother had had twins who didn't survive). On that evidence it was clear, I was going to be a single mother of not one but two babies.

'Knowing your luck it'll be twin boys as well,' my friend said, a bit too gleefully.

I started to feel more than a little bit alarmed. I wasn't sure that I could cope with one baby yet, let alone two. I called my mum looking for reassurance but instead drove her back to the sherry. Even my brother wasn't very calm about the idea of twins. I had always thought having twins was wonderful, but that was before I was actually going to have them. I would be a single mother of twins, without being able to get my huge double pram on the bus or into shops. Gosh, what if this meant I would never be able to shop again?

And how on earth would I afford it? I mean two of everything! I'd been worrying about buying one of everything just a week ago. And I would have to come up with two names rather than one, although actually that might be fun. Oh my goodness, I really needed yet another lie down.

The worst thing was that I had two weeks before my scan, which meant that I had two weeks of fretting. So, I decided to try not to think about it, and head back to denial, although I have to admit I did look at double prams on the internet which almost brought me out in hives.

My mother was very good at sending me care packages. I'd had wrist bands, my headache strips and home baked cheese scones. Yummy. So I came to look forward to my mother's parcels arriving.

The following day I got another one. It was two packets of knickers. Enormous knickers. I blinked as I looked at the label and then I pulled a pair out of the packet. I was a size twelve, only a couple of months pregnant, and despite my twins fear I wasn't *that* big. Two of me could have fitted in them. As my future flashed in front of me I felt sick, and clammy and ever so slightly agitated.

'Mummy, you sent me huge knickers.'

'I thought you'd need them. You should have seen the size of me when I was carrying you.'

'Mum, I am not planning on my bum being that big. Not ever.' I was verging on the hysterical.

'Well OK, but you are going to get big.'

'But there's no reason for me to get that big, I mean I'm going to be exercising and stuff. And the baby is in my stomach not my bum.'

'Oh well send them back and I'll change them.'

'I'm not really going to get that big am I?'

'I don't know, I was enormous. Although, I suppose I did eat cream cakes rather a lot with you. Oh and when I was four months pregnant I looked as if I was ready to give birth. I thought you might take after me that's all. Especially if you are having twins.'

Twins and now enormous knickers. How much more could a girl cope with?

I wasn't going to get all neurotic about my size; actually, who was I kidding? I hadn't been skinny since I was about twenty-four, and I was always meaning to go on a diet and do more exercise. I was guilty of talking about losing weight a lot rather than doing it. To cut a long story short I had far from the perfect figure to start with. I could blame my break-up for it if I really tried; I thought that being dumped from a great height would make me thin. But it didn't. Just sad and miserable. And wanting to eat crisps and cheese. I was a size ten girl in a size twelve body and hadn't had the willpower to sort that one out.

During my pregnancy I wasn't going to diet, but I wasn't going to gorge myself and become enormous (I swore to myself I would never wear those knickers). So I was eating relatively healthily with only the odd lapse, and I was exercising a bit as well. I was waiting for the three months to be up so I could do pregnancy yoga because I really liked yoga, but I had been swimming regularly and walking as much as I could. Oh and I was religiously using *Clarins* toning oil every day, rubbing it on my stomach (a friend of mine swore by it to keep those threatened stretch marks at bay). The plan was that I wouldn't put on too much weight this way nor would my baby be in any danger. But as I relegated the knickers mum sent me to the drawer I did fleetingly worry that my bum was going to be that big.

I had already had to start addressing the fact that there were certain clothes I couldn't wear, (actually quite a lot). My dresses which were either too tight for my boobs or made them look as if they would fall out at any minute. My favourite bras were no longer remotely useful, and I could wear my jeans but only below my stomach giving me a rather saggy builder's bum effect. I couldn't believe how I was less than three months pregnant and already facing a wardrobe crisis. I wasn't prepared to buy maternity clothes yet, not until I had the scan and so I was rather limited. Luckily I had some tops that hid my stomach and the jeans were OK if not perfect. Not needing those big knickers yet, that was for sure.

Single or not, the early days of pregnancy weren't easy for anyone I assumed. Not just the illness but the worry; I tried hard to be calm but I was also bit anxious about losing the baby which I knew would devastate me. There seemed to be more questions than answers, and every time I did answer a question another one would pop up.

Carrying a baby still felt like the most amazing thing I had ever done and I didn't want to get it wrong. But the fact it was so amazing meant that it could take a person over, and to an extent that would happen and rightly so, but my aim was for it to enhance me, not to become me. Does that make sense? In my world it did.

I had to go out to a new hotel bar one Saturday night. I was sick just before it was time to get ready and I was exhausted; the last thing I felt like doing was going but I said I would, and as I had barely left the flat after dark I thought I needed it. I pulled on a pair of leggings, a short but full dress and a pair of heels. With my hair straight and heavy make-up I looked OK, and not even pregnant.

It's funny how when you're trying to keep something quiet, you feel as if you're wearing a flashing neon sign. Not just my expanding belly but the fact I felt so terrible and at times struggled to string a sentence together. For someone who normally struggled to shut up, that was highly noticeable. But to be honest I found it easier to avoid people as much as possible, because I felt awful and also because I really felt as if my condition was obvious.

But that Saturday night I went out and sat down while my flatmate (the only person who knew I was pregnant) ordered me a lime and soda. With me being known as liking the odd (or lots of) cocktails, people wanted to know why I wasn't drinking. I was of course on antibiotics I said, very strong ones which also made me tired. For a particularly nasty urinary infection that was threatening to spread to my kidneys. I would even describe my symptoms if I felt so inclined. It was funny how people didn't tend to ask any questions and I almost believed I was taking the antibiotics myself.

The problem with this particular outing was that I didn't know that many people there and so I had to answer questions. Normally I loved questions, talking about my favourite topic (me), was something I was pretty good at. But suddenly with the exhaustion, and the fact I'd been sick most of the day, I just struggled. It was a good job my fictional antibiotics were strong as I slunk back on my seat, became largely monosyllabic, until just after midnight when I could finally leave. I had gone from being a bit of a party girl to wanting my slippers and bed. I was the most boring person I knew all of a sudden. Which was really quite upsetting. People made an effort to talk to me and I could barely respond let alone be at all witty or interesting. It was as if there was a different person sitting in the bar and I didn't know her. I worried slightly that being pregnant was going to eclipse my personality which couldn't happen, could it? I wanted the old me back again. But I felt too tired to look for her, even if I knew where to start.

I tried to tell myself that it was because I was so unwell that this was such a chore for me and after the three months were over I'd feel more like my old self. I wouldn't turn into an idiot or anything like that. I wouldn't become boring forever, would I?

Most of all I didn't want to think that for the next seven or so months I wouldn't want to be sociable at all. What if I turned into a hermit who had to wear enormous knickers? Perish the thought.

You should try not to let Pregnancy eclipse your personality but then pregnancy seems to have a personality all of its own.

Eight: First sight

I would lie on the bed, my best friend by my side. The screen would appear and I would see my baby for the first time, tiny, but there, and healthy and gorgeous. I would cry tears of joy. The sonographer would say that she had never seen such a gorgeous baby at this stage in its life and tell me how it was definitely going to be a genius child, but not in a weird way.

I'm only going to make a quick note about this right now as at that point it was too early to be thinking about the birth (I actually thought that when I was giving birth it would still be too early to think about it). However, all the books talk about a birthing partner and although I hadn't quite figured out what that meant exactly I thought I ought to have one. Most of the things I'd read assumed that it will be your partner, but as I didn't have one I needed to look elsewhere. I fathomed that a birthing partner was a very important role; you needed someone to be at the birth with you for support; they may or may not be holding a video camera; they needed to really like you in order to agree (after all I wasn't sure I liked myself enough to witness myself giving birth).

Basically I decided that I needed someone to keep me calm, be practical and someone I could shout at because facing it, it was going to hurt. Now of course the ideal person to shout at was the guy who got you in this predicament in the first place. Naturally, you were delighted to be pregnant and couldn't wait to have a baby but, and the big but, was that you had to go through labour. As I previously stated it was too early to be planning the birth, although apparently people had already devised a birth plan by that stage, (didn't really know what that was either), however I needed someone not only to shout at but to accompany me to my scan and generally be around to give me the support I would otherwise have if I weren't single. Simple.

Oh and by the way there was no way I required them to video the event. I mean honestly does anyone really think that's a good idea? Why would you want to watch it back? And when you invite your friends and family around for 'video night,' they really wouldn't be happy, trust me.

I asked my flatmate. She was one of my oldest and best friends and a terribly good person to shout at, although I hadn't done that before, but she was quite tough and looked as if she could take it.

'I'd like you to be my birthing partner,' I said. She smiled and seemed quite pleased.

'OK, great. What do I have to do?' It wasn't the time to tell her about the shouting.

'Don't know really but just being there would be great and maybe you could come to my scan with me.'

'Of course.'

After a while I think the reality sunk in.

'I'd be there while you're giving birth?'

'Don't worry about that, you can stay at the head end.' After all my birth plan, when I made one, would state that I intended to do exactly the same.

In the run up to my first scan, I was looking forward to and dreading it in equal measure. I desperately wanted to know that everything was alright, but I was worried in case it wasn't. My symptoms were still going strong, although I have to say the sickness was easing off a bit and the headaches weren't quite as severe. The tiredness or exhaustion hadn't abated at all though and I was definitely getting even more of a belly. My emotions were in turmoil. On the one hand I still thought I was having twins, on the other I thought it was all a huge mistake and I wasn't even pregnant. My thoughts were pulling me in so many different directions that I was convinced I would end my pregnancy mad, if I wasn't already totally certifiable.

What if they told me that it had all been a misunderstanding and there was no baby? I know I needed my head tested, but I veered between having twins to having no baby. Perhaps I was having a phantom pregnancy because I was told I couldn't have a baby. I was pretty sure I had read about women who put on weight, were sick and yet everything was in their minds. With my overactive imagination, that wouldn't be impossible. In actual fact it was scarily highly likely.

Just before the scan I was incredibly calm. I wasn't even sick that morning, which was good and I drank a lot of water because although I hadn't been told to I'd read somewhere you get a clearer picture with a full bladder. See, gold star pregnant girl yet again. As my flatmate and I entered the hospital I started to feel incredibly nervous, and I felt myself shake. She smiled at me reassuringly and I took a deep breath and then I felt really excited. The two contrasting emotions took battle for a while within me as I went to reception, and then stood in the waiting room. My name was called thankfully quickly. It was showtime.

As we went in, I asked if it was alright for my friend to attend, they said 'of course,' and in we walked. I was instructed to lie down on the bed, and as soon as I did I was gripped with terror. My whole body tensed and the lady with the stick (I think she is a sonographer but not sure), told me to relax. My flatmate smiled at me again reassuringly and we were good to go.

As she prodded my stomach we looked at the screen. Well my flatmate did, I couldn't bring myself to, nor could I breathe.

'One heartbeat,' the lady said.

'Not twins?' I stuttered.

'No, just the one strong heartbeat.' She smiled, kindly and then I did breathe and I finally looked. On the screen was something that apparently resembled a baby. I could just make it out when it was pointed out to me that although it was still small it was definitely there. My flatmate was quite excited and I was struck dumb. I watched it moving around on screen, the baby, my baby, was inside me. It was real, I wasn't totally mad. Once again I had no idea exactly what was going through my mind because the thoughts were rushing at a million miles a minute. I couldn't catch them at all.

I was over twelve weeks pregnant by then, all was OK, the heartbeat was strong and I was going to be a mummy. In real life. I had actually seen my baby, and I was totally overwhelmed.

We left, clutching the blurred photo which my flatmate said was clearly a baby but I was more inclined to see a fuzzy blob. I called my mum.

'Hello darling.'

'I've had the scan, everything's fine, I'm over the three month period and the baby is very active apparently.' I couldn't stop smiling.

'Oh thank goodness, so everything's OK?'

'Yes, all fine.'

'Did Charlie go with you?'

'Of course, she's here.'

'I hope they didn't think you were lesbians.'

'I'm sure they don't really care about that.'

'But you should have told them that you weren't,' she pushed. Mothers.

Having played the single mother idea over and over in my head, I had concluded that having a baby on my own was not that unusual in this day and age but still, thinking back to the waiting room I was the only one there with a female friend the others were all with men. Couples, they were all couples. I pretended to myself I didn't notice the reassuring looks, or hand squeezes that went on in that waiting room. I pretended to myself that I wasn't that unusual and more than that I pretended to myself that my baby would be fine despite only having one parent.

Perhaps I was more unusual than I thought although I desperately hoped that wasn't going to start plaguing my thoughts. I was lucky enough to be carrying a baby and so far everything was good, so there was no point in taking the joy away by worrying about what other people thought. I had a feeling that I would have to confront that issue at some stage but it wasn't something I wanted to do just yet. At the moment I wanted to bask in the utter glow of happiness I felt at the tiny little fist size thing that was growing inside me.

We went to have a cup of tea and Charlie and I were both getting excited. I bought a card and put the scan picture inside and mailed it to my mother. I wanted her to see her grandchild without delay.

And now, I knew that the so called 'danger' period was over and I was properly able to embrace pregnancy now and all that came with it. And boy was I sure that there was a lot that came with it. But for now I could celebrate. My first little milestone warranted a lovely cake with a cherry sitting right on top. No cream though, I still wasn't ready for the knickers.

The scan picture arrived with mum the following day. She phoned up and was excited although she likened my firstborn to an alien from mars. I took umbrage but she said you couldn't really see much but she was going to keep it so we could put it in the baby's album. She was so excited, I let her off the insult. She called me back later in the day to say that she'd shown it to my brother, who had cleverly held it up to the light and yes, it did look like a baby. Now she was properly excited, now that she could see her grandchild was going to be a baby rather than an alien. Is this a good time to worry about the gene pool? I fear it might be too late for that.

Motherhood is Love at first sight

Nine: The secret's out

The News that I was pregnant was followed by huge congratulations. Everyone felt as if I was very brave to be going it alone and offered up support. They said they knew I would be a wonderful mother and the child growing inside me was very lucky. Of course they also commented on how much pregnancy suited me and how absolutely gorgeous I looked. A huge celebration was had by all.

I was over twelve weeks pregnant and therefore I could tell people. There were still only a handful that knew as I had been really good at keeping quiet. And part of me was happy to go on keeping quiet. I certainly wasn't rushing for the phone. I would be lying if I said I wasn't worried about telling people. I knew my family and close friends would all be supportive but I was still feeling slightly unprepared for inevitable questions or people judging me. I think it was perhaps irrational to be quite so apprehensive, but my feelings were very mixed up still. I was thrilled now, really looking forward to the day I would meet my baby but I knew that this wasn't the way I wanted to have done it and there were unresolved feelings of guilt and worry that were still flooding my brain. There was still the ideal world floating around and my world wasn't quite it; well it wasn't it at all. My fantasies had been shifting as my reality demanded and still I was trying to reconcile them. I was happy with what was happening despite the fact that it wasn't happening in the way I had envisioned. But there was still this battle between fantasy and reality and I was still fighting within it. My world was far from perfect but it had to be perfect for this baby, so I had to make it so. Perhaps none of this made sense, but I had to make it make sense, and that was seemingly a tough call.

I was delighted to be pregnant now that I actually accepted that I definitely was and I was ready to look forward to having a baby, but I also knew that doing it alone might not be easy. I knew I wasn't alone, I had the most fantastic support around me and everyone who knew so far had been wonderful, but I wouldn't have the other person who made the baby around. Neither would the baby, which also made me feel sad, and guilty and inadequate. I was trying not to think too far ahead to when I would sit my child down and have 'that conversation,' or how I would cope without my mother's favourite discipline line, 'wait until your father gets home.' Honestly it used to really work with me. And instead of being upset that I took more notice of my father than her, my mother was just glad to have something that effective to use. But I wouldn't. I would be all the child had parent-wise and well, even at my best I worried that I wouldn't be enough, or good enough at least.

Although I knew that was silly or perhaps irrational, I did have moments where insecurity would strike me and almost make me feel breathless. I loved the little baby growing inside me, that wasn't in doubt, but I wanted to give him or her the best start in life and I had already failed. However, again that was something I couldn't dwell on, for now I had people to tell.

I was prepared to be bombarded with questions and what surprised me most was that people seemed to be divided into two camps; those who accepted what I said and didn't pry and those who were auditioning for the 2008 version of the Spanish inquisition.

The first camp, funnily enough comprised the people I was closest to. Everyone was surprised, or more accurately shocked. But once they'd got over their initial shock they were all thrilled. Some asked me if I was happy before extolling their happiness but that was fair enough. In actual fact it was wonderful telling these people because not only did

I love them but also their excitement rubbed off on me. They didn't pry, they just wanted to make sure that I was alright and that I was happy. Got to love those people.

The Spanish inquisition camp was another story. I might be exaggerating slightly as they didn't actually employ any torture methods but the questions that were fired were exhausting, intrusive and downright rude. But like a true professional bullet dodger I deflected anything I didn't want to tell, gave away everything I did and made up the rest. Although most of these people were friends they weren't my closest friends and actually they were people that I decided I would avoid as much as I could in future.

Four years ago when my father passed away I quickly learned who my true friends were. It was sad but it often took a tragedy to discover that, and actually there was nothing wrong with fair weather friends, especially in fair weather. But this was another time when I realised just who would be there to support me throughout my new journey and who would be waiting on the sidelines just to catch the gossip. And those who had caught as much gossip as they were clearly going to get were eager to pass it on. Which I guess saved me a job. But of course the news spread quite quickly and I did have to harden myself to that.

And that was one of the problems I faced. I've said before, I know who the father is but his identity isn't something I am prepared to reveal for various reasons (some legal, some moral) and I know that it's a conversation I have to have with my child at some point but otherwise I have to keep it private. It's not me being precious, rather practical I think. So what's left is speculation. And you can't stop people from speculating.

I was beginning to realise that I would have to be strong for the baby's sake. I had to grow more of a backbone and I would have to learn to tell people that they had no right to know more than I was prepared to tell them. For someone who hated confrontations, and avoided arguments most of the time this was going to be no mean feat.

But I did hear what people were saying about me. Luckily, again, said people weren't my closest friends, because if they were they certainly wouldn't be anymore. They were people who obviously had nothing better to do than gossip about me. I heard various things said about me and my pregnancy; here are some of the nicest:

- I was irresponsible.
- I had obviously done it on purpose because of my age.
- I probably had no idea who the father was.
- Poor child.

I tried not to be hurt by these comments but I was human and fairly (over) sensitive anyway. None of the accusations were true and I knew that in my heart, but still knowing that people were talking about me behind my back and especially saying that I was going to be a bad mother did cut me to the quick. I repeatedly told myself that I didn't care what people thought, but I did, and although rationally I knew that they couldn't hurt me and I would love this baby more than anything, I did shed tears over it, feel angry and confused. I even worried that everyone thought this about me and I felt incredibly insecure for a while. It seemed that I had a few hurdles to face and this was one of them. I knew that I couldn't let what some people thought get to me and I certainly wouldn't waste what little energy I had feeling devastated by their claims. However, it is easier said than done and I would be lying if I said that it didn't hurt me at all. I can't pretend that there weren't many nights where I cried myself to sleep; I was lucky that I was still so damn tired that it didn't take long.

But still gossip followed me, as whispers in the breeze. I heard some pretty hurtful things, and faced a few unfair allegations. I let people talk behind my back and I cried when I was alone. I felt sad for my baby though and worried that it was a sign of things to come. It added to my guilt. Was I really ready to be a single mother and would my child ever understand?

Being pregnant was time consuming enough without all this added stress so I really decided to ignore it and ensure I stayed calm and healthy for the baby. I booked to go home to my mother's for a week. She hadn't seen me since I told her I was pregnant and I am sure she wanted to feed me and I also booked a holiday. A week in Spain. I was just in the second trimester, so the most important thing was for me to take care of myself and 'the bump'. Because what scared me the most was that my baby would be affected by what people said. I know that sounds totally irrational as it was still safely tucked inside me but I felt that the personal attack on me was almost an attack on my child too. I guess because now we were a team and we were part of each other. And that realisation struck me. Whatever people said, or thought, I had my baby and he/she was far more important than anything they could throw at me.

The downside was the gossips; the upside was that the sickness had totally stopped. It wasn't sudden, but it had started to calm down after the scan. It was a gradual process. I would be sick less times a day. Then not every day, and then one morning I woke up and I ate three meals and repeated the pattern for the next few days and I knew I was over the worst. The headaches stopped at around the same time, although the tiredness didn't. It seemed I would be stuck with that for a while. But you know I could live with that, and one day I would learn to live with the gossips and ignore the bad press. Hopefully I would anyway.

Pregnancy can be tough; both physically and emotionally exhausting, but having a child growing inside you makes it all worth while. Sometimes you need to sit down and just remember that.

Ten: The second trimester

Are you going to find out the sex of the baby, they asked me in my yoga class. Oh yes, I replied. What does your partner think? They asked. Oh he's also keen. Suddenly my partner existed. He agreed with everything I said and thought, and had dinner ready for me after yoga. Healthy, organic and delicious. He was funny, handsome, practical and helpful. And after dinner he would draw my bubble bath and give me a nightly foot rub.

Now I was fully in the second trimester of my pregnancy (please don't ask me why they are trimesters, I think it's American, and neither do I know why there are three of them, but my book talks about them, and so will I), and everyone knew, things were moving along. So I treated myself to retail therapy, and invested in maternity clothes, buying from Top Shop and H&M, and I loved my pregnancy wardrobe. I was also really into elasticated waists, what a brilliant invention. I had managed to get a capsule wardrobe and I didn't wear baggy jogging suits unless going to yoga.

I'd started with my pregnancy yoga classes in my quest to be healthy and active and also they said it made the actual birth easier. And who wouldn't want that, even someone in denial about actually giving birth. Since my scan, I felt as if I could now be more active, so I still swam and I had a pregnancy yoga DVD which I would do at home and I went

to class once a week. In no time I would be glowing with health and I would be relaxed and calm.

I would get the bus to the class, and I looked forward to it, because I was spending so much time on my own it was nice to be sociable. I would walk into a room full of bumps of various shapes and sizes. We would all compare notes and then do some gentle yoga poses, and at the end we'd have some relaxation time. I didn't always fall asleep.

When I lived in Singapore I took a yoga class there. I went with a friend and the teacher taking the yoga class obviously decided on sight that I was the village idiot. Firstly she asked me, v-e-r-y-s-l-o-w-l-y if I spoke English. It went downhill from there. Although I established that not only did I speak English but I actually was English, she still insisted on addressing me as if I couldn't understand her and seemed to single me out. As she explained the principles of yoga she talked about what we shouldn't do. There was something about how yoga didn't discriminate, anyone could do it, even M-u-s-l-i-m-s, she asked me if I knew what a Muslim was and when I nodded, she still explained that the women wore headscarves. Then she went on to say that we didn't take drugs. She asked me if I knew what drugs were. Get the idea. On it went and all I could hear was my own confusion and my friend giggling at the back of the room. Finally she said that in yoga you didn't tell lies. I swear she looked right at me as if challenging me. I couldn't go back to that yoga class again, although my friend thought it was the funniest thing ever.

Anyway, the lady who took the pregnancy yoga class was always talking about what a wonderful experience giving birth was and how we would enjoy it. We should enjoy it. I didn't believe her, not for one minute and it made me think of my Singaporean yoga teacher. She would never have told us it was wonderful, she would have said that it would definitely h-u-r-t. I wondered if yoga forgave white lies though because it was sweet of her to try.

I guess the class made me feel less lonely. What was lovely was in that room we were all so excited and giggly; there was an energy that seemed to take over. We were all different but we were all carrying babies and we were all incredibly happy about it. It gave me a new lease of pregnancy life. Even when I could barely see my toes let alone touch them.

One girl was talking about her upcoming twenty week scan.

'Are you going to find out the sex of the baby?' someone else asked.

'No, I want to but my husband doesn't, so we're going to wait.' Then everyone started talking about if they were or weren't going to find out the sex. It came to my turn.

'Oh I am definitely going to find out,' I said. Which was true.

'What does your partner think?' someone asked me.

'Oh he's totally in agreement,' I replied. And thus, my fictional partner was born.

I don't know why I didn't tell them I was single, but I didn't and then my fantasy partner grew along with the baby inside me, I almost believed he existed myself. Once I invented him I couldn't take him back. I don't want to sound screwed up but I think because I had been subject to gossip I wanted to protect myself from it. And to be honest these women might all be pregnant but they weren't my friends, they were people I saw for an hour once a week, so I think I found it easier to invent a partner rather than explain why I was on my own. I probably underestimated them, but I didn't want to be gossiped about any more than I already was.

Perhaps I also got to, for an hour a week at least, fit in with what felt like normal. I was a normal pregnant woman, and there was nothing out of the ordinary about me. I probably wanted that more than I ever dared admit. I wanted, desperately wanted, to be normal.

I hoped my baby didn't grow up to be as insane as its mother.

There was a hairy moment when they were arranging the birthing weekend, where partners and cushions would be required, and I wondered if I'd have to hire a male escort (imagine booking that job), but then common sense took over and I just didn't go.

I was getting better now, I felt physically great, not even as tired, and I had started to relax into my pregnancy and even enjoy it. I didn't pay any heed to the gossips and I decided that if I was positive for my baby then that could only be a good thing. I needed to be strong and capable, and so I focused on my baby. I started reading magazines, thinking about prams and cots and although I didn't know the sex, names. I started building a little file of things I would need to buy, and as I loved shopping I even would pick up the odd thing. I made lists, I talked about the reality of having a baby, as my bump grew so did my confidence and my happiness. I realised that though all this, despite everything I was being given a chance. An opportunity to turn things around. It was like a new lease on life. After the past few years, after feeling that all I did was lose things, here I was gaining at last. I had the opportunity to be a mother and even if the circumstances were far from ideal, I would make them ideal. I might not be able to make my fantasies a reality but I could make my reality a new fantasy. It didn't totally make sense yet but somewhere deep down I knew it would. And when I went to yoga and I laughed and joked with the other mothers-to-be about my baby, and my imaginary partner, I knew that somehow this was my way of doing the best I could for my baby. In a way I hadn't even figured out properly yet, it was all about protection. Protecting myself and therefore protecting my child. I was learning to trust my instincts again. I was learning about love all over again.

So as I approached the twenty week scan which as far as I could tell marked the beginning of the end (or actually the third trimester of my pregnancy) I would sit at home in the evening, just me and my bump, watching my Dallas box sets and pondering the merits of names such as J.R or Sue Ellen, as I prepared to be a real life mother.

A mother tries to protect her baby from the moment she knows it is there.

Eleven: The Third Trimester

My baby girl was going to be an actress when she grew up. Not because I was a pushy mother but because she loved acting, and had inherited a natural talent from her mummy (undiscovered, of course). I would go to the premier of her first movie with her, wearing some divine couture dress and be so proud, because I had produced her. With this in mind I would, of course, have to come up with the perfect movie star name.

I remember people saying that when you're pregnant you become public property. It wasn't just a case of strangers trying to touch your stomach but people seemed to think they had a right to say what they wanted to you. I was in a shop one day and the shop assistant asked me when the baby was due.

'Beginning of November,' I replied with a bright smile.

'Goodness, are you having twins?'

Comments like this hurt. As you know I had already had a twin fear when I was first expanding but having a stranger basically say that I was big was really awful. And the shop assistant wasn't the only one. I had quite a few people comment on my size, as if that wasn't a bloody offensive thing to say to someone who was a bit body conscious anyway. In fact I went to my midwife terrified I was having a giant baby. My midwife, S, measured my expanding stomach.

'Your bump is the perfect size.'

'So I'm not giving birth to a giant?' My midwife was lovely but she did laugh at me quite a lot. Next time anyone said I was big; I would tell them that I was centimetre perfect, actually. No, on second thoughts I would just give them a dignified look and not respond, because people should know better and if they didn't then there was definitely something wrong with them. Very, very wrong.

My second scan approached and this was the one where I would find out the sex, and I couldn't wait. I was convinced that I was having a girl, but as one who has never been very good at surprises I needed know. I don't know why I was so sure I was having a girl but I was, as were most of my friends. My friend and I had even bought a vintage dress for the baby. I know that that sounds crazy but the dress was just too adorable, and once I had my tarot cards read and there was a strong indication that I would be having a girl, so it must have been true. I put the dress in a trunk I had bought especially for my baby, and couldn't wait for her to wear it.

I had a long list of names for my girl, none of which were Sue-Ellen as it turned out, and a very short list for boys, i.e. none. I know, from my yoga class that lots of people wanted a surprise when the birth came, but for me, being pregnant was enough of a surprise in itself, and bit by bit I was getting to know my child before it arrived. This for me was another step towards that. I remember when I was with my ex, harbouring dreams of having a conventional life, we had a friend who was pregnant and at that time I said that if I was going to have a baby I wouldn't want to know the sex. Well, I had definitely changed my mind. I'm not sure if it was because I didn't like surprises, or the fact that I was on my own but there was no doubt in my mind that I wanted to find out.

I felt by knowing as much as I could, I would be more prepared when the baby actually arrived. I thought that so much of life had been out of my control that anything I had control over, I would embrace, or actually cling onto as if it was a life raft.

A girl at yoga came to class after her twenty week scan and said that the baby was laying wrong so they couldn't tell her if it was a boy or a girl. I was horrified but as I spoke to more people I also heard stories it had been wrong. Apparently they don't guarantee one hundred per cent and if you're having a boy who is hiding his bits, he could look like a girl. Imagine, you've painted the nursery pink, and bought a pink pram (not that I would do that regardless of the sex), chosen a name, and then a boy comes along. So, of course now I had something else to fret about. What if they couldn't tell me? What if they did and they were wrong? Would it ever end?

I decided that if they couldn't give me a definitive answer I would go for a second opinion. I knew that I would have to pay for it and goodness knows I wasn't exactly rich, but that was how important it was to me. I guess it became yet another thing for me to be neurotic and obsessive about. I just hoped I wasn't passing these traits onto my unborn child.

My mother came to my second scan; she was very excited to meet her grandchild and I found myself caught up in her net of exhilaration. My baby had been very active, kicking away and moving, making me feel as if my stomach was constantly fluttering. It was such a comforting feeling; my baby seemed to be dancing, having a party inside me. She was going to take after her mother.

As lay on the bed again this time I was more excited than nervous. My baby was the right size and everything looked good as it moved around in my tummy. In fact the woman said that the baby was turning somersaults and showing off quite a lot. She was going to take after her mother.

'There's no doubt about the sex,' the woman said; I held my breath. 'It's a boy.'

'Are you sure?' I asked.

'Yes, look, he's got his legs above his head and his dangly bits are there for all to see.'

My son the exhibitionist. He was definitely his mother's son. A boy. Wow. I was a bit numb, because I really had been convinced it would be a girl, but not disappointed I don't think, no, I am not sure how to describe how I felt. At first there was a tiny bit of disbelief. Then there was the striking reality. There was a baby, and now that baby had more of an identity, that of a boy. A little boy with dangly bits and all was flipping around in my tummy.

All I could think of was what I was what the hell was I going to do with that dress?

My mum claimed to be the only person who knew that it was going to be a boy. She was utterly convinced apparently, although she hadn't shared that with me. She was chattering with glee as I clutched the two pictures of my boy and we went into town. I phoned everyone on the way to tell them and everyone was delighted. A few of my friends asked if I was sure, still unable to have been wrong about me having a girl. Honestly, it wasn't just me that was mad, all my friends were too. I was having a baby. I was having a baby boy. I welled up with emotion and stroked my stomach protectively.

My mum and I did our first shop for my son. She bought clothes, and blankets and rattles and anything else I would let her, I had to rein her in a bit (a lot). But as we picked out blue baby clothes, and little tiny vests I began to picture my little boy in them. Reality was thundering through me, stomping, and pushing fantasy out of the way at a great pace. But reality was great, and I let it carry on. And I fell even more in love.

I think it hit me a bit later, that the real reason I was so convinced I would be having a girl was that that was easier for me being a single mother. What I now worried about, (prematurely I know), was who was going to play football with him? Would I have to become more comfortable in mud? Take him fishing, (I am scared of worms and basically anything that moves), and 'boy stuff' like that? You see I was being terribly politically incorrect, and gender specific. I imagined me taking my little girl shopping, and doing her hair, now I was wondering if I could master the off side rule and climb trees.

But actually by the time we got home with bags and bags of shopping, I was so elated yet again. Because boys always loved their mummies and my boy would do so in spades. And his mummy would love him back.

My only remaining problem was the name. I like Raphael, but my brother pointed out that he was some kind of famous turtle, and who wanted to be named after a turtle? (I was thinking of Raphaella for a girl). I was stuck. So, I went to Waterstones and bought a coffee (decaf), and sat and drank it whilst reading the baby names books. This almost became a full time job. Then inspiration struck. I called my brother again

'Thom, what was that school friend of yours called whose name began with X?'

'Xavier.' I knew without thinking that his middle name would be for my father.

'Xavier Thomas Bleasdale.' My baby had a name.

At yoga, they were all really keen to know if I had found out the sex.

'Yes, it's a boy,' I announced with much fanfare.

'Wow, your partner must be thrilled,' someone said.

'Oh yes, he couldn't be more so.'

That was the only little fly sitting in my ointment. But never mind.

I had also made an extravagant purchase, well for me anyway, it was a calf and foot massager, this massive thing that you put your legs in and chose a setting and away you went. It was like my surrogate husband. It didn't cook me dinner, or buy me flowers but boy sitting there in front of the TV with my feet and calves being massaged made up for all that. I didn't mind that it didn't load the dishwasher and actually on the plus side neither did it leave the loo seat up or his clothes on the floor.

Despite naming Xavier, I still called him 'the bump,' mainly in case I changed my mind as I was fairly likely to do. I talked, sang (badly), I sat with my calf and foot massager, and the three of us became a family; albeit a very odd family.

A loving mother would never put her son in a dress, even a gorgeous vintage one. N.b. Christening robes are exempt from this comment.

Twelve: The Long Goodbye

My baby boy was growing inside me and would soon be ready to come out. It was time to be practical, as boring as that sounds. I would have to decide where to live and thought that the leafy suburb of Hampstead in London would be a good place. My mum would come and stay and I would be surrounded by friends. There were lots of prams always wondering around there. I would find a lovely little two bedroom flat, and then give birth in the local hospital. All that remained was my need for a pram. Bugaboos seemed very popular but which colour to choose?

I needed to be practical. My boy was growing as was I. I was really pregnant now, not quite waddling but not far off, and pretty happy with it all. But the reality was drawing ever closer and although I loved my life, and my friends I needed to do what was best for me and my baby. The truth was that I was still out of my depth and I needed to make a big decision in order to feel able to cope. I decided I would move back to Devon, where I grew up, and where my mum and brother lived, to have the baby and stay for the first few months until I felt ready to resume my life in London.

Because that was not in question. I grew up in North Devon, in the country, near the sea and although it is undoubtedly a beautiful part of the world, I didn't want to live there. I was a city girl. I loved the city and that was that. But for now the city wasn't going to be right for me. My mum couldn't drop everything and come to London, and I couldn't afford to get a two bedroom flat in Hampstead even if she could. My brother wouldn't be close by, and although my friends would be nearby they all had jobs. I had a very good friend in South West London who had one child and another on the way and I thought about moving near her but she had her hands full. What it came down to was that this single-mum-to-be needed her Mummy, and her mummy happened to be in Devon.

I told my friends I would be moving home.

'What will you do in Devon?'

'Go for walks and to the beach and stuff.'

'What will you wear?'

'What I normally wear.'

'You have to promise not to start wearing tracksuits and trainers all the time.'

'I won't.'

'And if you wear wellies make sure they are *Hunters*.'

'OK.'

'And don't buy an anorak no matter how practical they seem.'

'I promise.'

'And come back as soon as you can.'

'I will.'

I did go pram shopping. For me, the single biggest decision facing me now was what pram to get. There are so bloody many and I found it all really quite impossible to know which one was right. I went to a shop, alone, which was a mistake and felt so overwhelmed that I almost burst into tears. So, I researched, I asked people, I wished I had someone to do this with me. I didn't know what to do.

I felt silly, but it was times like this that it hit me I was alone. When I had to make a decision about things, I realised that no one else would share in that with me. Some said that I was lucky because I didn't have to argue with anyone but myself, however it terrified me, because I was so scared of getting things wrong. You might think, so what, it's only a pram but to me this was a huge decision. I wished there were only three available then I wouldn't have such a dilemma. Perhaps it became a bigger deal because it was slightly symbolic of my situation. Decisions now would be made by me, and proper decisions, not just what I would eat for dinner or what shoes I would wear, but what means of carriage my baby would have, and that was just the start. There was no room in denial over this so I resolved it by choosing the pram I liked the look of most. And it came in black.

For the rest of my baby needs I went with my best friend to John Lewis. In the baby department we got a woman to build me a list of all my practical needs. This was significant for me because I was leaving London, and therefore (I assumed) leaving the shops. My friend and I milked the last shopping trip for all we could. Firstly we made my baby list, and John Lewis assured me that everything would be delivered when I was ready. I loved that. Then we went for lunch. Then we shopped a bit for us and finally I bought my baby his first pair of *Ugg* boots. Because I might have had problems with the pram, and all sorts of other things but I knew my baby needed his *Ugg* boots. Footwear was something on which I was not in doubt.

I had a long goodbye. One friend took me to the Wolsey for lunch where I looked enviously at her oysters and Champagne and said I would soon be back for both with a baby tucked under my arm. I spent the weekend with my pregnant friend and her daughter, saying that soon the three children would play together. My two lovely best friends threw me a baby shower, which was afternoon tea, with a small group of very close friends where I was 'showered' with gifts and love, and friendship and they all wrote notes to Xavier for when he was bigger. This was when I realised I couldn't change his name, so he really was Xavier, although funnily enough it felt as if he had always been so.

It was hugely emotional. Not long ago these faces had been picking me up after my break-up, and I had done the same for some of them. And now, here I was, the size of an elephant, baby kicking inside me, saying goodbye until the baby was ready to meet them. And although I was on my own, single, my baby had the best family, because they were all here ready to wave me goodbye. But only on the condition that I promised to come back and that I didn't wear an anorak.

Friends can make the best family, and can save you from fashion disasters, apparently.

Thirteen: Oh no, not the shoes

In my bestelling book, 'How To Be Good At being Pregnant,' there is a chapter devoted to shoes. I find it really irritating that they tell pregnant women not to wear heels in case you fall over and hurt yourself. Apparently being pregnant can upset your balance but I don't see how it's any worse than after having a few cocktails. So I wore heels, and not necessarily killer ones, throughout my pregnancy. Of course there were days when I wore flats but if I wanted to wear heels then I would. And I did. And I didn't fall over.

It was my last visit to my midwife, S, for a while. She had been such a source of support to me throughout my pregnancy I was going to miss her. After going through the normal stuff she told me to lie down so we could listen to the baby's heartbeat. This always made me feel a bit nervous, just in case there was anything wrong. I couldn't bear for anything to be wrong. We started listening.

'He sounds like a horse,' I said.

'He does a bit,' she concurred.

'Please tell me I'm not giving birth to a horse.'

'You're not giving birth to a horse.'

'I'll miss you S.' I think she was secretly going to miss me too.

My flat mate was helping me pack my things up. I was taking what I needed home and putting everything else in storage until I got back. We had basically packed away most of my clothes as they didn't even remotely fit, and anything that I didn't see as essential.

I had a funny relationship with packing. I had packed lots of my things off to storage before moving to Singapore. When I returned home I was so distraught by the break-up that I hadn't bought anything remotely useful home and then I had to wait for over a year for my ex to ship my belongings back. I lost so much as well and I know they are only possessions but when you are striped of them, you feel more attached to them. Once again, I had very little and then I starting acquiring more things, which was what I did. And here I was packing them up again, although this time I knew I would see them again, but it did conjure up some old emotions that perhaps hadn't been fully dealt with. I was reluctant to let anything out of my sight, because of what happened in my not so distant past.

'Faith you can only take what fits into your mum's car, do you really need your Deco ashtray table.'

'Of course.'

'But you don't smoke.'

And so it went. Apparently half my essential items weren't actually essential, so they all got boxed up. Finally, saving the best till last we started on my shoes. I had only worn my heels a handful of times since being pregnant. Not because I worried about falling over, but because I was drawn to my comfy Cardigan *Uggs* which I lived in and my ballet shoes. I wore heels when I went out, which was normal for me but I went out far less than I used to. But I loved my shoes. I was a shoe girl for sure. I owned every series of *Sex In The City,* just to look at the shoes. I wanted Carrie's shoe collection more than anything, mine wasn't half as impressive, don't get me wrong. Anyway, I decided that I needed to try them all on, to have my last bonding moments with my other babies. After a few pairs I threw them down in horror.

'My feet seem to have grown,' I wailed.

'I've heard about that.'

'Really?'

'Yes you can actually go up a shoe size when you're pregnant.'

I examined my feet. They weren't swollen they were just bigger. I started to panic. I loved my baby but I also loved my shoes.

'Please tell me that they'll go back to normal after I've given birth.'

'Of course they will,' she smiled reassuringly. 'Well they might.' Oh God, I felt like crying. 'and in the meantime you can get some of those lesbian shoes. There's a girl in my office and she's pregnant and the only shoes she can wear are those.'

'What the hell are lesbian shoes?'

'You know *Crocs*.' I finally entered hell. Although I would like to make a disclaimer that I don't think people who are not straight wear Crocs, that was my friend and she is very politically incorrect and her views are not at all shared by me, but I do find the shoes unattractive, and I never want to wear them.

I lovingly packed all my shoes away, and kept the only shoes I could wear; four whole pairs I was left with. I then did as much research as I could into whether I could expect my feet to go back to normal so I could reunite them with my shoes. I couldn't find anything conclusive; it just made me more confused, but then I determined that if my feet could grow then they could shrink and so they would definitely go back to normal when my baby came out. They just had to. My whole shoe life was depending on it.

'Are you sure you're alright about this?' My friend asked as we sat surrounded by boxes. I nodded, tearfully. I was happy but I knew I'd really miss my friends.

'I know that I need to learn to cope, and I need my mum around. I need to do what's best for this baby.'

'But what about what's best for you?'

'What's best for him is what's best for me.' That was the only thing I knew with any surety.

I finished packing up all my stuff, and looked around. It felt as if I was in the middle of another ending, but this one heralded a beginning, as I'd said, this was a fresh start for me. Finally, after saying goodbye to things in my life that I didn't want to lose, I was saying goodbye and hello in the same breath. Therefore this was one ending that I was happy with. I was going home to my mum, to my family, to have my baby, to start my life as a single mum. It was a journey I had never anticipated, or expected, let alone foreseen, but it was a journey I was on. And somehow and in some way I knew that I could do this, I didn't exactly think I would find it easy, or that I would be the best but I knew I could do it and I would do my best. As I packed up my belongings and prepared to go to Devon to meet my child, I knew I was going to be alright.

What's best for the child is best for the parent, precluding wearing ugly shoes naturally.

Fourteen: The oldest teenager in town

I was in Devon, but my spirits were high. I missed my friends, even my yoga class but being with my family was where I needed to be. As I didn't know anyone, I found a local anti-natal class, where I met some wonderful, like- minded mothers-to-be. Unlike yoga I came clean about my single status but it didn't matter. They were all lovely and we became firm friends. And as our babies were due close together they would be firm friends too. When I moved back to London we would keep in touch because of course we would spend quite a lot of time visiting Grandma in Devon. It all worked out perfectly. And I would wear my lovely shoes again.

I was grappling to reconcile what was happening to me with how I had assumed my life would play out. I was readjusting my fantasies accordingly, (sometimes), but still the picture of the conventional family still sat inside me and I felt as if I had failed. I was the oldest teenager in town, and I couldn't help but think this is what I should have been doing at seventeen, not thirty-something. Single, pregnant and moving home to live with my mum. In my many fantasies that had never been one of them and that hurt me. Despite everything, especially my excitement about the baby (which was genuine), I still struggled with the conflicts of fantasy versus reality.

When I moved back to Devon I needed to keep myself busy, mainly so I didn't miss London too much, but also so I didn't worry constantly. A fantasist with an over-active imagination can sometimes think far too much and that wasn't always a good thing. I didn't want to think about anything negative, and I was practicing positive thought, actually quite successfully. I was reading about the laws of attraction and call me crazy if you like but I was making lists of everything I wanted for me and my baby, and I slowly began to trust that it would all be alright. But there were the same old fears and worries that tried to climb into my mind and I needed to ensure they didn't spend too much time there.

Instead, I turned my hand to being practical; I learnt how to assemble the cot and changing table, discovering a bit of a talent for flat pack furniture. I was a dab hand with my Phillips Head screwdriver and my Alan keys, and I had even stopped saying, 'who is Alan and why have I got his keys?' constantly. I am not saying it was easy but I managed to do it, and felt pretty proud of myself, you see I didn't need a man after all. I was almost feministic in fact.

I was eight months pregnant, bigger than ever, my feet still hadn't shrunk and I decided that as I was living back with mummy I needed to nest a bit for me and my baby. So, I painted my bedroom, or more accurately got someone to do it for me and I made a lovely nursery area for the baby as we would be sharing a room for a while. I unpacked our very few belongings and made the room as homely as I could. I also read that you needed to wash anything you bought for the baby despite it being new, and although I didn't know why, I washed all my baby's clothes and blankets. There was no time for dwelling on those negative thoughts you see. They had no place here. If I couldn't get rid of them and I certainly couldn't change my situation, you know suddenly get a husband and a house and normality, then I had to suppress them so I could stay healthy and more importantly, relatively sane for my baby.

I had heard about 'nesting' being a symptom of pregnancy and I seemed to have caught it. For someone who is normally about as domestic as a wild animal, this was something of a huge transformation. My mum was over the moon as I insisted on spring cleaning (my mum is ever so slightly less domesticated than me), and emptying cupboards, clearing things out and re-organising. I was a whirlwind of tidying and cleaning, unstoppable, although I didn't start baking or anything too strange like that. I threw out a lot of things, (my mum was a bit upset about that), but I was relentless. My baby was going to live in a clean clutter free house with lovely tidy cupboards.

I hadn't lived at home since I was eighteen when I went to university, so I didn't know anyone , but as I was only planning on being there for a short time I wasn't too worried about that. However, I did have to visit the midwife and although I missed S, she was very sweet and she sent me to 'Parentcraft' classes. I thought this might actually teach me how to be a parent but no, it was something to do with preparing for birth, a bit like antenatal classes, I guess but with a really silly name. Anyway they would give me some information which I may or may not need and it would be a chance for me to meet other mums-to-be, which actually I really wanted to do, as I said, I missed the sea of bumps that was my yoga class.

I arrived at the venue which was a Children's centre, and was directed to a room with chairs arranged in a circle around it. I was alone of course, and nervously took a seat. There were three other couples there and one girl who was with her mother. It hadn't occurred to me to take my mum but I did wish it had done. Or my brother, not that he would have agreed to come and as we look a bit alike that might have been ever so slightly weird.

I guess that's the thing about being a single-mother-to-be, if you take a friend (not that I had any), they think you are a same sex couple, if you take a male friend they will be assumed to be the father. And well if you take your mother, I am not sure what that says, although the girl there with her mother made it clear that her partner was unable to come along because of work, so we all knew she had one. But I was a big girl. I had got this far and I wasn't really that bothered about being alone, I was more bothered about being there.

The atmosphere in the room was strange; it felt unwelcoming despite the best efforts of the women who ran the group. No one really looked at each other, although of course I decided to study everyone. There was a young looking couple; she was very blonde with quite a lot of make-up on and he looked like Brian McFadden, circa early *Westlife*. He was even wearing a white shirt and black trousers and I kept expecting him to sing. I think I might have stared at him a bit too much. The next couple looked quite normal really, although they were both intently studying the floor. The mother and daughter were quite a combination. The mother had rings on every one of her fingers and was wearing more necklaces and bracelets than I owned. She jangled every time she spoke, it was quite mesmerising. The daughter looked so young that I fleetingly wondered if she was above the age of consent. The final couple also looked really young. The girl was so thin everywhere but her bump, which was annoying, and her partner, who turned out to be called Buzz, had REAL tattooed across his knuckles.

Introductions over, the two ladies taking the class started telling us about our birth options. It struck me that as I have always maintained I didn't want to think about the birth, perhaps I shouldn't have come. But it was too late, there was no escape.

The lady in charge asked us all what our birth plans were. They were met with silence. Honestly it was painful, so I spoke up.

'Well,' I said. 'Mine is pragmatic. I would like a natural birth but as I have no idea about the pain I am going to wait and see.' They commended me on my sensible approach and then asked everyone else. It was like pulling teeth.

'Well I had a cesarean when I had mine and I was knocked out. But that was a long time ago,' the mother said jangling louder than a Christmas tree. Her daughter was stubbornly mute. Brian McFadden's wife said pretty much the same as me and Buzz mumbled something incoherent on behalf of his partner. The lady of the normal (ish) couple then suddenly came to life, and explained they had ordered a birthing pool from the internet and were going to have a home water birth. It was the most exciting thing that happened in the two longest hours of my life. I nearly asked her if she was on a water meter but I refrained.

The ladies then went on to do their best to put us all off Epidurals by using lots of garden string and tying one of them up so in the end they resembled a packaged supermarket chicken. It wasn't very appealing, although I told myself in my very pragmatic way that you might get all tied up, but at least it won't hurt. They also tried to show us pictures which they insisted were very artistic, actually for a while it sounded as if we were in an art appreciation class rather than *parentcraft*, but as they were of women giving birth, I refused to look.

When the two hours were finally up, they told us what next week's class was. I vaguely remember it was something to do with more about the actual birth but I had stopped paying attention long before. I had already made up my mind never to go back again and this did nothing to make me change it.

I worried that this made me a bad mother but honestly does anyone need to hear this stuff? It didn't make me feel any better about giving birth, only worse. And the support from the others in the class just wasn't there. By the end still, no one looked at each other and still they only spoke when they absolutely had to. I might make some friends locally but they certainly weren't in that room. It made me feel lonelier than ever and I missed my friends even more keenly.

If I had been a little less in denial about the actual birth I might have searched locally for another antenatal class, I guess, but of course this is me we are talking about and I decided to cling onto the old cliché that ignorance is bliss. I was also pretty busy cleaning, and with my Alan keys, so I didn't exactly have loads of spare time.

With the books I read, the magazines that line the shelves of newsagents and the classes available there was massive amounts of information/support available for pregnant women. In most cases this is a really good thing, although I still maintained there was such a thing as too much information. But I think we all needed to be careful not to feel overloaded or to feel that there is no freedom of choice available. It was supposed to offer support, not tell us what to do. Some people want more support than others; we are all different and there is definitely no right or wrong in all this. It's hard sometimes but I tried not to feel too bombarded by it all, too overwhelmed, although I didn't always manage it. I also tried to remember that I was still me, an individual, not just a pregnant woman. Because we aren't all the same; we don't lose our identities the minute we become pregnant. Yes we are all going to give

birth to a baby, (hopefully a real one) but that doesn't make us all the same. You just had to be in that room to see that.

People queue up to tell you what to do when you're pregnant but you shouldn't forget to listen to yourself.

Fifteen: Motherhood means you actually have to give birth

*People say giving birth is painful but actually that wasn't my experience. It was quick, from the moment my waters broke until when my little boy popped out. No fuss, minimal pain, and I did it naturally. The moment that I first held my boy I cried tears of joy, I was euphoric, delighted and I didn't even feel tired. In fact the woman who delivered the baby said I was the best at labour that she'd ever seen. Honestly, I **almost** wished I had filmed it.*

Then it happened. I was totally unprepared, the contractions started a few days early, in the middle of the night, not that I knew they were contractions at the time. Everyone told me that first babies are usually late so I had told myself to prepare for an extra week or so. By this stage I was definitely ready to give birth. I was pretty big, and didn't fancy getting any bigger, I was really excited to meet my son, and I had run out of cupboards to clean. So in theory I was ready, but in practice I wasn't.

Don't worry I am not going to give you all the details of my labour (although it would be churlish of me not to furnish you with a few), but I was first aware of some pains which were a bit like period pains. They woke me up, and in my imagination I would have panicked but actually I was quite calm. At first I wasn't sure if I was in labour so I picked up my midwife pack and called the local hospital. They helpfully said it sounded as if I *was* in labour but as my contractions were quite far apart and my waters hadn't broken, I should take some *Paracetemol* and take a bath. This was about four in the morning and I thought I probably had days of this ahead of me, so I did as I was told. I sat in the bath but then that was uncomfortable so I went back to bed, but I couldn't fall asleep so I went back and had another bath, and I spent a few hours going from the bath to the bed and back again. To distract myself I tried to read but I couldn't focus, and then I would watch TV but there wasn't much on that that time of night, so that didn't work either.

I called the hospital again and said that I was actually in pain and they said that I should stay calm and call them again when my contractions were closer. Fleetingly I wondered if it would have been better for me to have actually paid attention to all that birthing stuff.

At six I finally managed to wake my mother with my stomping around and she asked me what was going on. I told her I thought I was probably having a baby.

'But we're not ready,' she wailed. 'John Lewis hasn't delivered.' I ask you.

I spoke to the hospital again, and they said they would send the midwife to me as I still wasn't ready to go in apparently. I felt as if I was being a bit of a drama queen but it did hurt, I can tell you. I called Charlie, my appointed birthing partner, at about half past eight in the morning.

'I'm just going into work, is everything OK?'

'I think I might be having the baby.'

'Oh shit, what should I do?'

'Well nothing right now. I'm waiting to see the midwife and then I'll let you know but it will probably be ages yet so don't panic.'

'I'm wearing my Alexander McQueen boots.' She sounded worried.

'Perfect birthing partner footware. Oh, I get it you're worried about them getting ruined.'

'Well...'

'Don't worry you can always take them off.' I told her I would call after seeing the midwife. I was still relatively calm and proud of my rationality, but I was rapidly going off the idea of a natural birth.

The midwife arrived. She examined me and said that I was about half way there, which was a real surprise and I was allowed to go to hospital. I called Charlie again who this time did panic and said she would get straight to the train station and see me at the hospital. It was actually happening, my friend was on her way and my boy was on his way.

My mother drove me to the hospital still fretting about John Lewis, and in the car I called and texted other friends to tell them I was in labour. For some reason I wanted everyone to know, and I guess it also distracted me a bit. I was a little scared, a little excited and in a lot in pain.

I got to the hospital where a birthing pool had been booked, which I thought I would try to use for pain relief if nothing more. The pain was really getting intense but the midwife told me that my contractions weren't that strong. They felt bloody strong to me, and I told her so in no uncertain terms. I hopped into the birthing pool and they bought the gas and air over for me.

'You might want to take your knickers off,' the midwife said.

'Oh yeah.' I felt really stupid.

The water and the gas and air weren't as effective as I would have liked so I said perhaps I would have an epidural after all. Who cared if I looked like a supermarket chicken? Not me. But the lovely midwife said that I was due to be examined in about an hour's time so to sit tight. Like I had a choice.

I think I was a bit confused because my waters hadn't broken and although I was assured that this was fine and everything was alright, I was still convinced that I had hours ahead of me and I didn't think I could cope with those hours. I shouted that the gas and air was rubbish before grabbing it and sucking on it as hard as I could. I think I swore a couple of times. My mum was behind me and she was trying to be reassuring, I wasn't paying any attention, but bless her for trying.

When I asked Charlie to be my birthing partner I told her that she could stay at the head end, well while I sat in the birthing pool I stared intently at the ceiling. I didn't want to see what was actually going on so I didn't look. I was tired and cranky and a little bit like a child having a tantrum.

'I want an epidural,' I said, pleadingly to the midwife. She went and got another midwife to come into the room.

'I've really had enough,' I reiterated to her. 'I want to get out and have an epidural, please.'

They exchanged glances.

'It's too late for that,' she said.

'OK then I'll have Pethidine.' I was being oh so reasonable.

'It might be too late for that. Do you feel like pushing?'

My baby was put on my chest straight away, and all I felt was an overwhelming relief that he was here, he was alright and he was mine. My mother cried, she saw her grandson being born and she was all emotional. I didn't cry, however, I held him and there was a tiny bit of disbelief that there was a real baby in my arms mixed with euphoria that it was over.

As I was cleaned up and the baby was weighed and then given to my mum to hold, all I remember was huge elation, and then everyone in that room told me how beautiful my boy was, but it was as if I didn't need to be told because I already knew. I was so proud, and elated and exhausted but also a little bit smug because I had had a natural water birth. Even if it was accidental.

I held Xavier so tightly, and I studied him, and he was truly beautiful. He slept in my arms and everything felt as if this was how it should be; everything felt right. I kissed his tiny head and I whispered to him; 'I will give you all I can, and you are going to have an amazing life, I promise you that.' Then I felt emotional. It hit me that I had a baby and I was a mummy. It was real.

After a short while, they said we were ready to go up to the ward and bizarrely they gave me a supermarket shopping trolley to take all my things in. There we were again, the odd family. Myself, my mother, my baby and a supermarket trolley carrying our bags; somehow it seemed pretty normal.

It was the beginning of my son's life and actually it felt, if not the beginning, then definitely the start of the most important chapter in mine.

The realities of motherhood start here.

Sixteen: The celebrations

This was how I had always envisaged my birth experience. I would be sitting up in the hospital bed in a beautiful nightdress, hair resplendent, holding my beautiful baby and sipping a glass of champagne. There would be photos taken as my handsome husband looked on proudly whilst he discussed how many carats my eternity ring would be.

Xavier was six pounds six ounces. He came into the world with a mop of dark brown hair and looked like a darker version of my brother, and a bit like me. My mother had arranged a private room so that I wouldn't be in a ward where my baby was the only fatherless one, and as I hadn't thought of that, I was grateful. It wasn't the celebration of my fantasy but it was one filled with love if not champagne but then I was breastfeeding after all. I had started grieving for the conventional family I craved when I was pregnant and I knew that it would take a long time before that would pass, if ever, but right now my only certainty was that my son deserved the best and I needed to do the best for him.

I was still exhausted from the birth, and all the emotions that were swimming around my head, I still wasn't sure what my thoughts were actually doing. But reality had given me the most wonderful gift and I held that tiny bundle in my arms and I am not sure what exactly I felt, but it was good. No, who am I kidding it was wonderful.

When settled into our room I heard a really loud click clacking along the corridor and Charlie burst into the room. She had missed the birth, luckily for her, but she was one of the first people to meet my son, and I was so glad that she was there. I think it had taken her about four hours from London and she was sure that she would be here to see Xavier being born. However, Xavier wasn't waiting for anyone, something I was pretty grateful to him for.

'I can't believe I missed the birth,' she said as she held my boy.

'You were lucky, I'm not sure it would have been much fun for you.'

'He's gorgeous.'

'Thank you darling.'

'Why have you got a supermarket trolley in your room?'

My son might have been gorgeous but I was not. The problem Xavier being early was that I had a hair appointment booked for the day after he was actually born. My idea was to leave it to the last minute so I would have lovely hair for the photos. The photos of me holding my baby and gazing lovingly at him, which for now would remain firmly in my head. Like some kind of diva I banned anyone from taking a shot of me and as I was looking scary they all complied. I looked like a wild banshee woman in actual fact, so there were only photos of my baby. I then asked my mother to re-book my hair for as soon as I was out of hospital. If I could have I would have got my hairdresser to come to my room to cut and dye my hair there.

It was all a bit of a blur, I texted friends and family announcing Xavier's arrival, I managed to speak to a couple of people. Due to my accidental water birth, Xavier's body temperature was a bit low, so although we had had cuddles, he had to spend time in a hot cot to warm up. But I did manage to feed him and felt really quite proud of us both as he latched onto straight away and breastfed without an issue for either of us. So, my son was already showing signs of genius. From the birth which I wouldn't exactly say I enjoyed, but it could have been a lot worse, to the fact that he breastfed easily. I changed my first nappy and I felt a little bit overwhelmed, but at the same time like a real mum.

It's quite funny the way that you spend nine months preparing for the birth, and some people a lot longer when babies are planned, so why when you have a real baby in your arms does it seem to take you by surprise. I knew I was having a baby, I'm not that insane but when I held him and looked at him I was still a bit taken aback. Is that just me? Perhaps we shouldn't explore that.

I lay on the bed, my baby next to me in his cot, with my mum, Charlie, my brother Thom and nephew Rob who had come to meet the new arrival, oh and of course our shopping trolley which sat by the bed on my other side. I had flowers and cards and phone calls and it was a celebration. I had done it, I really had. I had given birth to a beautiful, healthy baby boy and he was gorgeous. He also slept through most of his first day, so clearly very clever too.

I can't talk about immediately feeling overwhelmed with love because I was overwhelmed with everything and it wasn't until a day or so later as Xavier Thomas Bleasdale and I were in the hospital bed, watching the American election results, that I looked at him and I thought, 'I know you.' It was an historical moment in more ways than one.

I stayed in hospital for three days, because I was in a private room they didn't seem in a huge hurry to get rid of us and I wasn't going anywhere. With the help of a nurse I gave Xavier his first bath, and he moaned a bit but wasn't too bad really. I was petrified of dropping or hurting my tiny little boy but I didn't, thankfully. The thing was that I had help and support, when Xavier didn't seem to be feeding someone taught me to tickle his feet and he started feeding straight away. I felt secure there, or as secure any first time mother can feel at least. The midwife who had been with us throughout the birth came up to visit us which I found really touching, and the staff kept popping in to check on us. I had heard horror stories about NHS births and aftercare but I cannot praise my hospital enough. They were brilliant, quite frankly. The only issue was that they thought Xavier looked a bit jaundiced, and we had to test him, but the results meant that he didn't need treatment, so we were given the green light to go home.

Suddenly I felt stressed. I would have agreed to stay in the hospital until I was sure I knew what I was doing. That might have been until Xavier was ready to start school mind you. But I called my mother and told her that she could come and get us. I got dressed for the first time since before the birth, feeling almost surprised that I hadn't lost loads of weight, and got Xavier ready. I looked enormous in my maternity clothes and Xavier looked so tiny in his baby grow, which was too big for him. I put his little scratch mittens on and a hat to keep him warm before wrapping him in a blanket. I worried because all Xavier's clothes would be too big for him; I didn't want him to start his life looking anything but dapper but he definitely needed to grow a bit first. And I needed to shrink a lot.

My mum arrived with the car seat/carrier. It was still in its plastic bag.

'Mum, I thought you might have taken it out and figured out how to fit it,' I pointed out.

'Oh, I didn't think of that,' she replied. I scowled. This was something I would have done had Xavier not decided to make his appearance early. I couldn't find any instructions, and although strapping Xavier in was easy I had no idea how it went in the car. My mother suggested asking someone in the ward but I got all paranoid and worried that if they found out just how incredibly stupid we were they wouldn't let us out of the place until I passed some kind of exam in car seats.

I walked out carrying my baby in the car seat, trying to look confident, my mum pushing the supermarket trolley, which if I was honest, I was going to miss, and I felt like a bad mother for the first time in my short motherhood.

Slightly hysterical we finally managed to strap the seat into the car. I am ashamed to admit that for the first time I swore in front of my son. It was pretty simple but it took me ages, and of course the minute we got home, my brother opened the back of the car seat and pulled out the instructions. But I had got my baby home safe and as I walked round the house I introduced him to his first home, and I did feel quite emotional and proud and amazingly relieved. I might not quite have been *Supermum*, but I was going to be. I put Xavier to bed in his cot, because the Moses basket hadn't been delivered, and he looked so small and the cot looked so huge. That first night he wouldn't settle; I wasn't sure if it was because the cot was so big, or because it was first night nerves so I put him on my chest and we slept like that. I know people say you shouldn't, but as I slept with my baby for the first time in our room it just felt right. I would do what I could to make sure that everything was right from now on. I might not be perfect but I would try and try and try until I was as near to it as I could be.

Motherhood means being the best for your child, and doing the best for your child.

Seventeen: Baby days

My son and I bonded. We spent the early days blissfully together, and I was getting slimmer and slimmer every day.

Fantasy and reality almost managed to hold hands for a while. Apart from the fact that my baby weight didn't drop off. This actually surprised me. I remember reading about people who after giving birth were slimmer than ever and I decided that that would happen to me. Apparently it was a hormone thing. You see I would be a size eight in no time without actually doing anything. I was actually really excited. But alas that didn't happen; luckily I didn't order those size eight skinny jeans. In fact breastfeeding was making me so hungry I was actually putting on weight. Did women actually put on weight after giving birth? No one ever told you that that could happen. I was more than slightly perturbed.

I had been meaning to be careful about my eating after giving birth but of course when you're breastfeeding you can't really diet or do anything drastic and I barely had the energy to walk up and down the stairs let alone hit the gym. But what I wasn't prepared for was just how hungry I would be. I ate constantly, and when I wasn't eating I wanted to be. I still wasn't having any caffeine or alcohol or anything too bad for the baby, so my diet was healthy, but it was also huge. When you're pregnant they tell you not to eat for two and I didn't, but when breastfeeding I think I was eating for about four. It was beyond annoying but I couldn't do anything about it. Well apart from eat, of course.

When I got home, I had no idea what I was doing. Really, what first-time mother does? From the first few days I knew I could feed my baby, change his nappy, and even bath him but that was all I knew. To be honest I don't think I needed to know much more than that, but at the time I felt a little bit lost and fearful I think, because as Xavier was taking his first breaths, I was taking my first steps into motherhood, and like a child learning to walk I was a little bit tentative, a little bit wobbly and I fell over a fair few times. I called the maternity ward so many times I lost count; I pretty much had them on speed dial. And each time I called they offered me reassurance. Which was what I needed.

Despite the fact that I was still huge, and just so you know my feet didn't seem to have shrunk, I did get my hair dyed and cut so I looked a hundred times better, and felt it too. I can't speak for everyone but after giving birth I was still exhausted, a little vulnerable and terrified about doing the wrong thing. And I felt dowdy and fat. So just getting my hair cut made a huge difference and I was pretty overjoyed about such a small thing. And my mum was pleased because she was allowed to take photos of me and Xavier at last. But only from the neck up, of course.

There was so much information out there for new mothers, as there was for pregnant women, and it could be a bit too much. Just as not knowing what to do felt overwhelming, the advice could be too. Which is why I avoided the internet and just relied on the maternity ward. I also realised that I needed to start to trust my instincts. We definitely have maternal instincts and women hundreds of years ago must have relied on them, I'm sure. Although thinking about it they used to rely on wet nurses too, so perhaps my argument doesn't work. Anyway, it was hard to take that leap of faith, and believe that I would know what to do, but I was going to try. I hadn't always listened to my instincts, I had sometimes fought them, but now, now I needed to let them guide me more than ever.

It's true that much of what early motherhood consisted of was instinctive. I instinctively breast fed, and seemed to know much of what Xavier needed when I stopped panicking and listened to him and myself. I knew when I could put him down and when he needed cuddling. I knew how to bond with my baby, and I knew how much we meant to each other. I knew how much I loved him, because I did. Despite all my fears and worries, I fell more and more in love with him by the minute and I didn't know love could feel that way.

When I was in Singapore I had some Asian friends who practiced confinement after giving birth. I might be a little sketchy on the details but in effect they would stay in bed for about six weeks after the birth, which is apparently the time it takes for the body to recover. I remember one friend telling me she didn't get up to shower or bath even, but had bed baths. Which I didn't quite understand because that would really upset me, but there was definitely something in the rest of it. They often moved their mothers in to do anything that needed doing and they stayed in bed taking care of their babies. I did ask my friend what the role of her husband in all this was and she looked a bit surprised and shrugged. I think she thought he had already done his bit, but that's a whole other story.

In a way it was really quite genius and I did find myself following their lead a bit and I kind of made up my own type of confinement. I did shower, and I did go out but I also spent a lot of time in bed, with my baby in my arms or sleeping in his Moses basket next to me. When he was sleeping, I would either sleep or read and I felt properly rested. And believe me I knew I was lucky. Because I had moved in with my mother she did everything for us both. She washed, cleaned, cooked, ironed, waited on me hand and foot, and did all the shopping. I really had nothing to worry about but my baby and myself. She would bring me breakfast in bed, and any other meal I wanted. She would take care of Xavier while I showered or bathed, so I didn't have to rush. And this way, lucky old me didn't feel too exhausted because I was getting enough sleep. I would recommend anyone giving birth to borrow my mother, although thinking about it, I still need her.

But, as I said, I didn't stay in bed *all* the time. We went for walks; Xavier was just this tiny little bundle wrapped against the cold Devon wind all cosy and gorgeous in his pram. I took him to the beach introduced him to the sea, and to see the countryside, and he slept through most of it.

Every day, I was visited by a midwife, who would check me and check Xavier, and apparently we were both doing brilliantly. I had to take him to the hospital to have a heel-prick test when he was about five days old, but I wasn't worried about that and the results all came back fine. Soon the midwives, who weren't always the same, said that I was doing marvellously, so I was passed on a health visitor. I won't explain the difference between them or what the roles are because I'm not quite sure. But my health visitor came and weighed Xavier, chatted to me and was again, quite impressed with us both. I got a much needed ego boost, as I was told how well I was doing as a mum. Xavier got cooed over which he seemed to enjoy.

On her third visit however she noticed my confinement.

'You seem to be in the same place every time I come here,' she pointed out. I was going to explain how bed was the best place for me and how much I loved it but she didn't look as if she would entertain that.

'I do get up, honestly, and we even go out. It's just a coincidence,' I protested; a bit too much.

'Well that's great; instead of me visiting you, you can bring Xavier to the weighing clinic every Tuesday.' As she furnished me with information, it seemed confinement might be over a bit sooner than I would have liked. But I didn't like to argue, because after all I was trying to be the perfect mummy.

My health visitor was lovely, and everyone who saw me was aware of the fact that I was a single mother. My goodness, it hit me that I really was a single mother. For so long I was getting used to being a single-mother-to-be, and now I was no longer to-be. It sounded weird, even after all this time. I wasn't sure if I would ever get used to it. The health visitor, however, gave me bags of support and encouragement. After the birth there were moments where I felt vulnerable but then I had so much help that I didn't panic and I didn't feel alone. I was blessed and I will always appreciate that.

Quite a few hours of the early days of Xavier's life were taken up with feeding – I breastfed, but wasn't overwhelmed with breast milk. In fact on the advice of a website I bought a box of a hundred breastpads.

After I stopped breastfeeding I gave ninety-eight of them to a friend of mine; the other two I had used as coasters.

I was also trying to express milk pretty early on because I wanted my mother to be able to feed Xavier (seriously I had my poor mummy doing everything), and also for him to be used to having a bottle from the start so he wasn't too used to my boobs. But of course I was still determined for him to only have breast milk. I was like *Express Dairy*, only I would sit there for an hour just to get a tiny bit of milk. I used an electric breast pump and it was possibly the most undignified thing I ever did apart from the actual birth. I got quite determined though and after ages, I would get enough for one feed for Xavier and then I would have to have a rest because it was bloody exhausting. But I kept going because not only did I like the idea of Xavier having a bottle but also I was told it would stimulate my milk flow. I am not sure that this was actually true, mind you as my milk continued to just trickle out.

My genius child fell into a routine pretty quickly. He fed every four hours; he slept the rest of the time. He didn't cry very much, only when he wanted something. He was such a contented baby on the whole, and I didn't even do anything to make him so. Of course after reading my 'everything you need to know and stuff you don't' pregnancy book, I had moved on. I read all the books about how to get your baby onto a routine. I felt out of control many times during my pregnancy and this anchored me. I believed that if I could get Xavier onto a routine I would cope better because I would know what I was doing. Especially as I wasn't naturally the most organised person ever.

I had friends with children and I had heard (and seen) the routine vs no routine debate and all I decided was that I needed to do what worked for me. So I wanted a routine, but not the rigid Gina Ford one, more of a routine that had room for flexibility. I read a variety of books before Xavier was born and I picked out the bits that I wanted and ignored those I didn't. I had even made notes. I was actually quite neurotic about it. I needed to feel I would have some kind of control over my new life and this seemed to be the best way to get it. I had toyed with the idea of feeding on demand and thought that that seemed like a really bad idea, I wanted him to have regular nap times, although not necessarily having to be in his cot at home each time. Oh I was pretty pleased with myself because I had it all worked out before my baby arrived. I really was going to be *Supermum*.

Then Xavier came along and I forgot everything I had read. I was so mesmerised by my baby that I kind of let him take over and tell me what he needed rather than vice versa. Also, when babies are newborn they really do mainly sleep and eat, and the routine develops as they do. It might not have been perfect but we were slowly working out a way that suited us both. So I shoved my notes in the cupboard and let Xavier tell me what he needed and thought that as long as it was healthy I would carry on. I employed the same theory I had to my birth plan; I would be pragmatic. I realised that the fundamental mistake I made when I was pregnant was that I thought my baby's routine would be what worked best for me, but it needed to work best for *us*. Because it was about the two of us now. That was all it was about.

Although my child was genius, he still cried though. He wasn't a big crier, didn't cry all the time but in the evening, just before I wanted to put him to bed he would cry, wrenching his little tiny legs up to his stomach, screwing up his face, and really telling me he wasn't happy.

'It's colic,' my mother said. What is it with my mum's generation and colic? I had researched it and colic was actually pretty rare, and it lasted for hours. Xavier would cry solidly for about thirty minutes before settling. So I put it down to trapped wind, stomach ache, and I gave him a dose of *Infocol* before the evening feed, and massaged his little tummy until it passed. This happened most evenings, and although upsetting, I always knew it would go away and he would feel better. It lasted for a few weeks I guess, and then just stopped as suddenly as it started. I have to say though that there is nothing more upsetting than listening to your baby crying. I felt a desperate need to fix everything and I felt inadequate if I could not. Welcome to motherhood. And when they are tiny I believed they did cry for a reason, it's their way of communicating. I'm not child expert, and I don't claim to be but I was getting to know my child and whether he cried or screamed I knew that he was trying to tell me something and my job was to listen to him.

People say that if you pick your child up as soon as they make the tiniest of murmers you are making a rod for your own back. Maybe, but with Xavier I wouldn't immediately jump every time he made a noise, because sometimes he would stir and then settle himself, but if he wanted some attention then I would give it to him. After all I still demand attention and there is nothing wrong with attention seekers, in moderation of course.

Largely I think the early days were a bit of a beautiful and tiring blur, a steep learning curve of trying to get to know my child, finding our routine and our feet. At the same time as wondering if I would ever see my feet again. (Looking doubtful).

If I had to sum up this time it was a time of nurturing. I nurtured my baby and my mother nurtured me. It was the perfect circle of mother-hood in a way, complete with soft boiled eggs and marmite soldiers.

Motherhood is being wise enough to take the best from your mother and apply it to your child.

Eighteen: Loneliness comes in all shapes and sizes

Everywhere I went I made friends. Or more accurately Xavier and I made friends. We were like the most popular kids at school, and we were inundated with invitations to play dates and coffee. I still missed my lovely friends but soon we would be reunited and until then we had some lovely new friends to play with.

I believed that I coped very well with the early days and even enjoyed them, but I also suffered lots of new mummy insecurities, fears, worries and I had huge moments of doubt as to whether I was doing the right thing or not. I often wished I had a partner, someone who shared responsibility with me, someone I could ask when unsure and who would give me an answer or at least debate with me. My mother was wonderful but she was a Grandma and didn't really want to be seen to be telling me what to do and actually she wouldn't have got much thanks if she did. But although I never stopped appreciating my family I did feel as if something, or perhaps someone, was missing. And I was sad about that at times.

Xavier was the most adorable baby and I was totally in love, besotted and in awe of him. I know every mother says the same, or at least they jolly well should do. He would look around at everything and I almost looked around with him. Wherever we went it was as if he was looking at the world through new eyes, which was exactly what he was doing. He would stare at me and I would stare back, as much as he liked looking around, he also maintained eye contact which people commented on. In this way he seemed to win everyone over. He smiled quite early (and no, I would say, it was not wind), and I would smile too. He looked as if he knew so much; there was wisdom in him; I know I sound quite mad but really that was how it felt. It was as if *he knew.* I would stare at him, as he lay in my arms and I wondered what he would be like as he grew, what he would be when he was older, and I knew I had no idea, which was as it should be. As I looked at him I saw a world of possibility; as I looked at him I saw the future.

I would fantasise, of course, and in each of my fantasy's Xavier would change the world in some way. Of that I felt sure, because he had changed my world. I am sure every parent shared this feeling with me, I was far from unique. I don't mean I mapped out his future in a pushy mother way, or that I intended on living out my unfulfilled fantasies through him. Let's face it; if that was the case I wouldn't want him to be a rock star, just someone who managed to have a pretty ordinary conventional life. You know, finding someone to love who is reliable and good, getting a secure job (civil service springs to mind), two kids, a family estate car, maybe a Volvo...

But thinking of my boy I knew that I would tell him all the time, as I did when he was in my tummy, that he could do what he wanted to do, be what he wanted to be and I would do everything in my power to help him believe in himself the way I already believed in him. That was my job. It was early days but it was as if I had known him forever and I couldn't remember life before him. He had been here a short time, but it felt as if he had always been with me. I was happy, oh so happy, but I did suffer degrees of loneliness.

I think that was fuelled by self-doubt, and the fact that I didn't really know what I was doing, at certain times I would feel worse than at others. It was a strange dichotomy, I was happier than I had ever been, but there was sadness there too. I was coping, actually I was more than coping, I was getting to know my baby and he was getting to know me and the world, but that didn't mean that everything was great. I had to separate the joy my baby brought me with the fear I was also experiencing. Fear and isolation.

What I needed was some support from people who were doing what I was doing. I needed other mothers. Before I gave birth I always maintained I wouldn't become a mummy bore, in the way that I didn't want to be a pregnancy bore. But let's face it I had become a pregnancy bore, so it was only right that I would become a mummy bore. Only I couldn't really because I didn't know other mothers to be a bore with. Of course I spoke to friends and family but I missed seeing people, just having a coffee, I missed gossip and really I missed my girls. I wanted them to be around me but they weren't and that was something I had to accept.

Since my health visitor made me go out, on a Tuesday afternoon I would go to my local town, treat myself to a nice lunch while Xavier slept, then we would do some shopping, before I took him to the clinic to be weighed. The health visitors were always really welcoming and I would normally get a cup of tea made for me, and we'd have a chat while they cuddled and cooed over Xavier, who wasn't the biggest baby, but was putting on weight steadily. Tuesday afternoons made me feel civilised, as if I was in the land of the living. While at the clinic I was told about a breastfeeding support group that was held every Friday morning. It was at one of the local children's centres and you could drop in and stay for two hours or less depending on how you felt.

They also gave me a newsletter which listed all the groups they ran. There was quite a lot. There was a single parents group, (or lone parents I think was the correct term), but I didn't want to go to that. I didn't feel that I needed to join a club for single parents, and I am not knocking it, because I am sure they offered support that was very valuable to many people. I just wasn't interested. I wanted friends and I wanted to meet other new mothers, and I really didn't care if they were single or not. Also, it said that a meal was provided, which I felt stereotyped a bit, and after all I was trying to lose weight.

My confidence was still quite low, and I was slightly nervous about this new social foray as it was held in the same place as the Parentcraft classes, but I really did want to start mixing with people so I decided to give it a go. Because I was a pretty terrible driver, (it had taken me five attempts to pass my driving test), when I lived in London I just didn't drive, the same in Singapore. In fact I hadn't driven properly for about ten years. And when I moved to Devon I wasn't planning on staying there so I still had no intention on driving. Which meant that my mother had to drive us everywhere because most places were too far away to walk and I couldn't fit my pram on the bus. My mum was my chauffer. I had to call her my chauffeur otherwise I felt as if I was being taken and picked up from the school disco. I couldn't help but yet again feel like the oldest teenager in town. She said she didn't mind but as she was doing everything for me, I felt more than a bit guilty. Not guilty enough to actually get behind the wheel though.

I felt very nervous walking into the room for the first time, carrying Xavier in his carrier. The room was full; there were a sea of mothers with their babies. I sat down and someone went to make me a cup of tea. I smiled nervously at others around the room, people seemed to know each other already and yet again I felt like a fish out of water. But I wasn't, because I had the right accessory with me, a baby, as did everyone else. I took a deep breath, and one of the mothers, who had a baby girl started talking to me. It was weird, the relief was immense. I almost thanked her. I felt some of the loneliness melt away. A few of us swapped notes, and conversation flowed. I could ask about things that had been bothering me and I felt less and less alone. At some point most of us got our breasts out. Xavier slept a bit, fed and then got passed around as the organisers wanted a cuddle with him. He didn't seem to mind as he was cooed over yet again. I think I felt human again, and although sitting in a room full of women breastfeeding might not seem exactly normal it felt normal.

There were, of course, a couple of unnerving incidents. There was one woman who had a baby who turned out to have been born on the same day as Xavier. I thought this gave us a common bond but she kind of blanked me after that revelation. I put it down to shyness, but I found it a little rude. Also, there was a crèche next door for older children and one of the women talking to me was a volunteer support worker who had breastfed all of her four children. I was impressed until one of her children appeared from next door, reached for her mother's top and started feeding. She was four. I know that you are not supposed to judge but I found it downright weird.

I know that breast milk is best for your baby, we are told that enough, but if I hadn't stopped before, then I certainly would when my baby got teeth. I really didn't plan on going on any longer than that.

The following week I went straight to my new friend E, and we sat down with our babies. The group followed a similar path, but this time I felt more confident so I was able to bring up something that had been bothering me.

'I really don't like breastfeeding in public,' I said. Some of the girls said it didn't bother them and others sympathised with me. You see, it wasn't other people that had made me feel this way; I just really didn't like doing it. I didn't mind too much in the group but when we were out and I needed to feed Xavier, it stressed me out a bit. Sometimes I would even rather sit in the car and feed rather than a cafe. And I hadn't had a bad experience, or anyone be rude to me, I was just incredibly self-conscious. Even though I had clothes on which meant that I wasn't exactly flashing, I just couldn't relax or feel at all comfortable doing it. They told me of a child friendly cafe in town which seemed to be full of breastfeeding mothers at various times. I did try that, but I have to admit to never feeling totally OK about it. Apparently I wasn't exactly earth mother material.

I don't think I was the best, or the most natural breast feeder in the world, that was for sure, but I was trying. I think perhaps it's OK to admit that I didn't really enjoy breastfeeding. I didn't hate it either, I just did for my baby, which made me feel good, but I wouldn't have won any breastfeeding awards. And Xavier was still exclusively breastfed, although he was only a month old, so I'm no where near as good as the mother of four, but hey, I was doing alright. I might not have loved doing it but I was doing it, because I was still trying to do the best for my bubba. People say it is the most natural thing in the world, but I have to be honest and say I didn't feel that way. I remember seeing my mum feed Xavier with my expressed breast milk in a bottle and they

seemed to stare at each other through the process. That, to me, was a lovely bonding moment between them. Despite my personal feelings about it, I kept going, and I was also secretly hoping that it was going to make me thin, although still no signs of that either.

A friend of mine was getting married in early December. Xavier was only four weeks old, but I was determined to go. I expressed milk as much as possible, (blimey I did feel for those poor cows), so I could freeze it and take it with me. Mum was going to look after Xavier while I went to the evening party. I even tried on the dress and I had planned on wearing, which fit me (it was stretchy), although I did look a bit elephant-like. The wonderful news was that I tried on a pair of my favourite heels and they fit me. My feet were normal again. It was cause for celebration. But for the rest of me that hadn't shrunk, I went into town and bought some control pants, and some control tights, so when I tried the dress on again it looked better even though I couldn't really breathe.

We were all set; I was going to see my lovely friends again. Then something happened. My lovely chilled out baby who fed only four hourly wanted to feed all the time turned into a monster. He was constantly routing for my breast, and he was fractious all the time, I hardly got any sleep, and was totally exhausted. I called the maternity ward (still had that speed dial), and they said it sounded as if he was going through a growth spurt, which usually lasted for four or five days. Four or five days of constant feeding and no sleep. Suddenly I realised what new mothers talked about when they said they were exhausted. Well I had only got enough milk expressed for his usual feeds and with the lack of sleep I knew in my heart there was no way I could go to the wedding. Apart from the fact I could barely stand up straight, I couldn't risk Xavier not having what he needed. I thought about taking Xavier with me but I would have to breastfeed the whole evening and in the end I realised that it wouldn't work as I wouldn't be able to relax.

I was totally disappointed, and cried over the fact I wouldn't be going. I didn't resent Xavier, well actually I told him he was a bit annoying, but I was tired, and that made me feel emotional, and despite the fact my mother was still serving me better than any butler, I realised what utter exhaustion felt like. However, it did pass and at least I guess the good thing was that Xavier got to grow a bit.

In the middle of this I went to another breastfeeding group, and I had never been so grateful. My new comrades had been through growth spurts and totally understood how it felt, how hard it was, and I felt still shattered but normal. As I fed Xavier yet again, I thought that at least I wasn't the only one going through this. I didn't ever feel totally lost, because I had Xavier, but I felt a little out at sea sometimes and this group had become a bit of a lifeboat for me.

My baby's first Christmas was approaching, Charlie was coming down to Devon to spend Christmas with us, and I was really looking forward to having one of my best friends with me. I was determined we would have a lovely Christmas and things would be better than ever. My baby's first Christmas; I could hardly believe it.

We had had a bad run in previous years. My father got ill at Christmas; my relationship broke up at Christmas; my brother had pneumonia at Christmas. It was hard for someone who loved Christmas but I have to admit Christmas hadn't been exactly kind to me in the past few years. Santa Claus owed me that was for sure. This year, however, was going to be different. This year I had Xavier.

Despite my up and down moments there was no doubt that I was a mummy now. A proper one; a real one. I loved Xavier so much and he was undoubtedly the best thing I had ever done, even if I hadn't actually meant to do it. I still had my expressed milk that I had frozen for the wedding I couldn't go to and I planned on using that, because although I hadn't had a drink yet, I wanted Champagne at Christmas, because this year we had loads to celebrate.

Motherhood, parenthood, is a club, you might not like all the members, you definitely won't be like all the members, but you all share something unique.

Nineteen: This year it will be different

Christmas was magical this year. We woke up to loads of presents. Xavier didn't really know what was going on but he smiled a lot. We drank Champagne toasting our future, Xavier's future which was all our futures. We had a delicious traditional lunch, followed by a walk on the beach. There was a lot of sparkle that day; everything sparkled. It was a perfect Christmas, and it even snowed.

Just before Christmas 2008, I was getting this motherhood thing down pat. I had a very limited social life, which was better than none, I was gaining confidence in myself and I told myself that whatever I did I would strive to be the best mother I could be. That was all I could do. Xavier had already given us so much. My family had a new lease of life, having been swimming in grief for the past few years, we still missed Dad, but this baby had given us hope, I guess, he had waved his magic wand over all of us.

My child wasn't yet two months old, so he probably wasn't really into Christmas. However I was. We bought a tree and decorated it, and I shopped, which of course was my favourite past time ever. We went to Exeter and bought presents, mainly for myself actually, although I did buy things for Xavier too. Despite Xavier not being the biggest baby, he was growing pretty well and was now able to wear the clothes I had bought for him before he was born and those given to me by friends and family who all had impeccable taste. He was already a pretty snappy dresser.

Before Xavier was born I maintained it was harder to buy clothes for boys than for girls and the ranges available seemed more limited. But I searched as did my friends and Xavier looked pretty gorgeous at all times. He also had his *Ugg* boots, and his *Vans* with skulls on them, so his footwear collection was also pretty cool. My mother's friend had also knitted some lovely jumpers and cardigans for him, they were quite old school and, he had a very cool wardrobe. I know you might think I was mad but this was important to me, and I was dreading the day when he demanded *Thomas the Tank Engine* shoes. It almost kept me awake at night.

I took Xavier to the clinic for his weekly weigh.

'Do you think he looks a bit jaundiced?' My health visitor asked.

'I thought that was just his complexion,' I replied.

'Well it's nothing to worry about, but it wouldn't hurt to have a test.'

'OK.' I wasn't worried at all. I think that Xavier had a bit of an olive complexion, so as I went to see the GP, I was fine. The GP examined him.

'Not sure, he might be but I wouldn't really think so. Anyway, let's just get him tested to be sure.'

It was a bit of a stupid process, because then I had to take Xavier to the hospital for a blood test. They took blood, my baby screamed, and I was just frustrated by the whole thing. At this point I still wasn't worried; I really good at positive thinking, and although it was late for him to have jaundice, it wasn't uncommon, and apparently it was more common in breastfed babies.

The test showed he did, indeed, have jaundice (my complexion theory was blown out of the water then) and further tests to find out the cause were ordered. I took him to the hospital before picking Charlie up from the train station on Christmas Eve. Still I was told not to worry, and I figured out that they weren't keeping him in so it couldn't be that serious. When they called me late on Christmas Eve to say that there was an abnormal thyroid and liver result I began to worry, although I was still told not to. The doctor told me that they wanted me to bring him in to see the consultant on Boxing Day. I worried further. This was Christmas, if it was nothing to worry about then surely it could wait until after the holiday. I finally worried.

I came off the phone and cried, my mum tried to hug me but I shoved her away and went and grabbed my baby. I looked at him, and he looked at me, there was nothing wrong with him, there couldn't be because there couldn't be. There just couldn't be. He was all that was good in my life; therefore he had to be OK. My tears dried up and I fed Xavier, I put him to bed, I had dinner with Charlie, and although it wasn't quite the celebration I was hoping for, we still tried.

By the time we woke up on Christmas morning I had put the worry behind me, well I had buried it anyway. This wasn't denial though, because I knew there was nothing really wrong with Xavier, and I had to keep believing that. We opened our presents and Xavier remained resolutely unimpressed with the proceedings. He had more presents than all of us put together, there was so much, I swear my brother was jealous, and I would have been but then I got to open them. We had lunch, and then played a game, which was guess the celebrity, and it was farcical because my mum and Uncle Ken had no idea who anyone was. My mother tried to give Ken a clue when his celebrity was Ewan McGreggor.

'He likes trains.' Funnily enough he didn't get it.

Charlie had Madonna to guess and she started asking questions. Suddenly there was a bit of a smell and she jumped up screaming.

'My hair's on fire!' We all looked, it was actually on fire. She hopped around like a bunny, patting it down and quickly she put it out. Boy it really stank though. She threw her Christmas hat down and had a bit of a tantrum, we all tried not to laugh but failed. She refused to play the game after that though.

After lunch we took a long walk down to the beach, with Xavier sleeping soundly in his pram. It was all as it should be, the actual events of the day were as I had imagined them to be. Only I didn't feel it. I stayed strong, I believed. I was positive, and I held onto my positivity as it was my only life raft. I also held onto my baby. I didn't want to let him go, not for one minute.

It was far from the way I imagined Xavier's first Christmas as the cloud hung over us. I think I went through the motions and I think I survived it, but I didn't enjoy it. I told myself that by Boxing Day this fear would be gone, I would be told that whatever was wrong with Xavier was minor and that it could be sorted out easily, but until I was told that I was terribly unsettled. I did drink the champagne, because it was Christmas but my first drink since I had found out I was pregnant threatened to choke me. I drank it but it was felt flat and there was no celebration in my heart that day. My baby's first Christmas was ruined with worry and fear.

This year it was supposed to be different, but not in the way it was. Santa Claus still owed me.

The minute you are a mother you start worrying about your child and I don't think you ever stop.

Twenty: Everything changes but you

Xavier and I had to go to the hospital on Boxing Day which is annoying but I was determined to be brave, strong and positive. A very handsome doctor greeted us (luckily I was wearing make-up) and sai that although we were told there was a problem with Xavier's thyroid and liver, it was only a tiny issue and here was some medicine and it would all be fine again. We were told we could now go away and enjoy Christmas. The handsome doctor asked for my phone number; I thought it might be slightly unethical but then I wasn't his patient was I?

On Boxing Day instead of having a lazy morning followed by eating leftovers and a tin of *Quality Street,* we went to the hospital yet again. I had been there so much in the past few days where my baby was pricked and prodded, that it depressed me to walk though the doors. I met Dr. P. Dr. P. was fairly old; actually he had treated my brother when he was a baby and my brother was now thirty, so he was very old. But he seemed OK, and he was trying to speak to me kindly. He told me that Xavier needed further tests for his thyroid and liver.

'He had the heel prick test and that came back normal,'

'Nineteen times out of twenty the issue would have showed up,' he replied.

'Right well are you going to do the tests now?'

'No. We need to do a couple of scans. One will be in Exeter and one here.'

I was beginning to resent having come in; it seemed that he wasn't actually doing anything apart from telling me they needed further tests; I had come here for reassurance and that wasn't happening. He examined Xavier and then he looked at me, lopsidedly, in what I took to be a concerned way.

'I'm afraid I think we need to test him for Down's Syndrome.'

People talk about the world stopping. Time standing still. About things falling apart. My story wasn't straight forward but I hadn't expected this. I was a single mother, I was a good mother, and my son was beautiful and healthy. I can't remember breathing, although obviously I did.

'But he's a perfectly healthy baby,' I said to Dr P, who now reminded me of a cranky old man trying not to be cranky. I almost stamped my feet as anger began to creep into me.

'Actually he's not.' I wanted to kill him. I have never felt such animosity toward a person ever. I gave him the bitchiest look I could muster, but if he noticed he pretended he didn't. I felt nauseous. I looked at Xavier, he looked fine to me; he looked the same as always. He looked like my baby, the baby I gave birth to. The baby I knew.

Things were fuzzy, my head was fuzzy, I just remember a big ball of fear that started in my toes and crept up my entire body. I don't know if I could hear. My mother was in the room with me but I don't remember if she spoke. I can't properly describe how I felt at that moment, but it was something so alien, so horrible that I never wanted to feel that way again.

Dr. P started to explain that he was fifty, fifty as to whether my son did indeed have Down's Syndrome. Xavier didn't have many of the physical features apart from his eyes, which I thought were almond shaped and just like my brother's were when he was a baby, oh and apparently a gap between his big toe and the rest of his toes which I really couldn't see, so I dismissed that. I wondered, fleetingly if Dr. P was crazy. Dr. P told me that he was normally eighty to ninety percent sure when he ordered the tests, and that he hoped that he turned out to be completely wrong. Perhaps then, when he did turn out to be completely wrong, I could force him to retire.

I wanted to ask him if he enjoyed putting the fear of God into people at Christmas, if he really couldn't have just kept that fifty bloody per cent to himself. I wanted to ask him if he had any idea what he was suggesting with those careless words. I wanted to tell him that he might have won awards for being a good doctor but clearly they were wrong. I didn't say anything though; I just clung to the other fifty percent like the clingiest limpet.

Because I couldn't contemplate it being the other fifty per cent. There was no way.

He couldn't do the test then either, so I had been dragged into the hospital on Boxing Day to be given the fright of my life and told that we wouldn't have the answers for days, and that we needed to go back yet again to have more tests. It was shit, and I hated Dr. P with all my might. I looked at my little baby and my heart broke. For him, and for me. For us.

I walked out of the hospital with my baby in my arms, sobbing my heart out. I had cried a lot in the past few years, tears were almost part of my family, but I had never cried tears like these before. Never.

No one could believe it, not my brother or my mum. We had known Xavier for nearly two months, how could we not know this. When we got home I took to my bed, like confinement all over again but without the smiles, or the happiness. Christmas, even if it had begun, was well and truly over.

Once again you find the kindness of people when disaster strikes. My mother called the maternity ward and spoke to the midwife who had delivered Xavier. She came straight out to see us. She held Xavier while I cried, she said that she didn't think he had Down's Syndrome but she also let me wail. She couldn't make it better, but she did offer some comfort.

Somehow I managed to function. I fed Xavier, I bathed him, I even took him out for walks, although I cried pretty much the whole way. My tears were angry, they were bitter, they were sad and they were afraid. But, until I had to go back to the hospital for the tests, life went on. Because if I had learnt one thing, that was it; that was what life did.

And Xavier had the same needs as he always did. He needed feeding, changing, bathing, loving. Xavier hadn't changed in the slightest, but everything else had.

I took Xavier for his Chromosome test. I had to wait to take him for his scans, which were to be in Exeter hospital, a forty-five minute drive away from us. I cringed when he cried as they poked and prodded him. I yet again, resisted the urge to kill Dr. P. If there had been a cliff handy I would have definitely shoved him off of it. I fed Xavier, I bathed Xavier, I held Xavier. I cried, and I slept. I don't remember anything else but fear.

I stupidly went on the internet but that just scared me further. I couldn't possibly even entertain that he had Downs' syndrome, I still had a fifty per cent to hold onto. But I will admit this: I would open up the internet and search, then close it down, and then open it, and then get scared and close it down again. This became a bit of a pattern. It was almost like when I watched a horror movie, I always kept one eye shut or hidden behind a cushion.

As people rallied around me; my family, the health visitors, the midwives from the hospital, and the one friend that I told, they were all sure that there was no way my baby had Down's Syndrome. Someone pointed out how alert he was; and he was. Also, my health visitor had told me to put him on his tummy, (tummy time is important, apparently), and he would sort of object and by the time we were at this stage he had learnt to turn himself back onto his back. So not only was he physically able, but he also knew what he didn't like. Ergo, he was smart, I knew he was smart from the beginning. He breastfed, which babies with Down's Syndrome can't do, I was told. Everyone who spoke to me or visited bought me a gift, a reason why Xavier was definitely not going to have Down's. I even went to visit my GP who said that his guess would be no, my boy was fine.

I took each reassurance and held it dear. No one but the stupid Dr. P, and maybe some other stupid doctors, thought that there was anyway that Xavier had Downs' syndrome. I just had to get through the test and the results and then we could get on with the rest of our lives. The way I had always planned. I was going to the same place;

I was taking the same route. I just had to get past the next few days before I could get back on track, and put this nightmare well and truly behind me.

But I was angrier than I had ever been. After everything I had been through I didn't feel that I deserved this fear. Was I being tested yet again? Hadn't I been tested enough? I never want to sound like a victim because I don't believe in that, but it was hard, oh so hard. The past few years had really pushed me to my limits. I had fallen down more times than I could count and I had always got up again. I had painted a red-lipsticked smile on my face and fought my way back every single time. And now, this. This was a step too far for me. I had never been so afraid, so confused so lost and bereft. I was scared for my son, and for myself, I was scared for both of us.

I cried buckets, and my mum had to help out more than ever, because I needed propping up, but Xavier didn't cry any more than usual, he fed and slept and smiled and gurgled. He was the same baby as he was before Boxing Day, before Dr. P. I looked at my son and I saw Xavier; that was all, and I would have known if there was anything wrong with him, and I knew, in my heart, in my mother's heart, that he was absolutely perfect.

Everything changes but you.

The fear you experience as a parent is a fear in a league of its own.

Twenty-One: My commitment

My child will be happy and healthy. He will live a full and wonderful life. He will be handsome and clever and funny. He'll be successful and will change the world. He will have a sparkling personality. He will do whatever he wants to do with his life, and I, his mother will do whatever it takes to ensure he can.

I would not contemplate any other life for my child. So far I had been pretty much re-adjusting each fantasy to accommodate reality. Not always, of course, I still had fantasies to reach for, but I was taking reality into account but I couldn't do that now. My fantasies, my best friends threatened to desert me. It was a very dark time for me; my darkest hours.

I looked at Xavier, and tried to find the answers, but I could not, although really I could, if that makes any sense. He was Xavier; he was my baby, my lovely little baby. I cried. I clutched him, and I cried. I wouldn't accept that Xavier being ill or having Down's Syndrome was in anyway a good thing for anyone concerned. I had committed to him more in the last few days than since he was born. I loved this little one more than I could express, and I would do anything and everything for him. That was my job as his mother. But I needed him to be OK.

I took the decision to tell no one, apart from immediate family and one of my closest friends. I was responding to an instinct, one that I still don't fully understand. I didn't really know how I felt and also I was still holding onto the fact that I believed, in my heart, that Xavier was fine. I didn't want anyone else to worry and I didn't really want anyone to feel sorry for us, or look at Xavier differently. I also didn't want to have to talk about it to lots of people at that time. After all it was all going to turn out to be a storm in a teacup and then everything would be back to normal and nothing will have changed. My thoughts and feelings were on a roundabout in my mind. Good, bad, scary, happy, all spinning in a way that I had no control over.

One of the only people I told, my very good friend who was in Australia at the time, suggested I write down what I wanted for my child. While we waited for more tests and more results, I did this, my commitment to my child, for the life I wanted for him and what I would try to give him. This is perhaps the single most important thing I did, because I wrote it, through tears, from my heart.

Darling baby Xavier

One day when you are old enough to read this you will know, if you know nothing else, that your mummy has always loved you and will always love you. I will give you everything I can, but love is the most precious of my gifts and it is unconditional. But also this is my commitment to you, as your mother, for your life. This is what I want for you more than anything.

I want you to live a healthy and full life (with no restrictions or hindrances). For you to be strong, happy, loved, loved, loved, and always feel confident in that. I want to ensure you have the best education and the best opportunities so that when you are ready to decide what you want from life you will have been equipped to make that choice. I want for you to see the world, and experience the richness that life has to offer if you go through it with your eyes wide open.

I want you to know that you can be whatever you want to be, do whatever you want to do, and I will always give you my full support with whatever that is, with whatever you choose. I want you to believe in yourself the way I already believe in you. I want you to know who you are and always be proud of who you are, because I am proud of who you are.

I want you to have a father, but a great one and one who loves us both, who is deserving of us, and I will now try to be open to meeting a man who can do this, and who we, in return, will give so much to. I want you to be worry free, and to have a childhood that you can enjoy. I want to shield you from the bad things in life but also ensure you are aware of the realities. I might not always be able to prevent your tears but I will always be there to mop them up. I want you to be loving and kind to others and through teaching you about the harsh realities of the world you can always know how lucky you are. I want you to be so, so handsome, which you already are, because your mother is a bit shallow after all.

I want everyone to love you, and to appreciate all you have to give. I know, already that you are an amazing person who will enrich the life of anyone you meet. I want you to be surrounded by good friends and family, so you never feel alone. I know that you might not be able to be free from fear, but I will teach you how to cope with it, how to cope with good and bad in life.

I am also going to write stories for you, so you feel that the world is full of stories, and you will learn to use your imagination, and understand the beauty in fiction.

I want to give you all this and more, the earth the moon and the stars, and I want you to be healthy most of all, to be amazing, to be able to make your own choices, stand on your own two feet, and most of all I want you to learn independence, and confidence, as well as knowing you will always be loved and cared for.

With all my love, always, mummy xxxx

With all the fear going on I finally focused on my son. I hadn't forgotten him because I was taking care of him but the fear had engulfed everything. Writing this to him, brought back the realities of my baby, and his life. It allowed me to focus on him for a while, not the tests that we were facing. He was still smiling away, he was such a happy baby, and I tried to be happy too. As I wrote the commitment I felt some of my terror melt away because when I saw it, in black and white, I knew that it was my son's future here and I was, in large part, responsible for that future. I couldn't afford to spend all day crying, I had to believe that it was all alright because Xavier deserved that. He deserved a strong and positive mother and that was what I was desperately trying to give him.

Still, it was the hardest few days of my entire life.

On top of the emotional, there was still all the medical stuff to deal with as well. On the way to Exeter to take him for his thyroid scan I had to take him back to the local hospital here to have a line put in. My new arch enemy Dr. P was there.

'I've got bad news I'm afraid,' he opened with. I visibly shook, because there was nothing more I could cope with. 'I need to test your thyroid to see if he inherited it from you.'

Perhaps bedside manner wasn't actually something they taught him all those hundreds of years ago when he was at medical school. I imagined having a baseball bat to hand and swinging it at his head. As he took blood from me I made a wish that I did have a thyroid problem and that Xavier had it from me and that would be the end of that.

I have to say that Dr. P seemed to be backtracking a bit as well. He told me that an under active thyroid could cause problems that are the same as some of those found in Down's Syndrome. I don't remember everything he said, but I did take his gift of sounding unsure and put it in my pocket with all my other bits of hope.

As for Xavier, it was awful, as he lay there on the bed looking so tiny. Dr. P couldn't find a vein, so it took ages, and he screamed and I wanted to scream with him. Then when they finally got it in, they put his arm in a splint and wrapped it up and it looked horrible. They were going to inject him with radiation so that I would have to wear gloves to change his nappy for a couple of days. I wanted to snatch my baby away and tell them to leave him alone but I couldn't because then they would probably have called Social Services. I let them do it to Xavier but I felt guilty that I couldn't stop them.

Next we went to have a scan on his liver, and then Dr. P gave me Xavier's pills which he would have to take every day for the rest of his life. For my two month old baby, thinking about the rest of his life was pretty daunting. It was all hell. If it wasn't for Xavier, I would have thought I was in hell, actually. But I still had my beautiful little boy and I clung onto him, radiation and plastic gloves or not.

Before we left, Dr. P, told me that he would phone me next week with the results from the chromosome tests. I wanted to tell him not to bother. I didn't need them; I would say, no thank you that's alright, just keep them to yourself. But I said nothing.

We drove to the other hospital where they injected him with radiation and then tried to make him lie still while they photographed him to see if he had a thyroid. The lady held his head and I held his legs but he wouldn't stay still.

'Can you get him to go to sleep?' Someone asked.

'If I could I'd be a pretty happy mother,' I retorted and gave them a look. They told me that in that case they couldn't guarantee that the scan would have worked and maybe we'd have to come back. I gave them another look.

In my imagination I felt like Uma Thurman in Kill Bill. With my trusty sword I would take down Dr. P, and then the scan people, and then anyone else who got in my or my baby's way. One thing I was sure of was that Xavier and I were both fed up, he cried and I joined him.

I gave Xavier his first thyroid medication. It was in pill form which I was told to grind up between two spoons then give him on a spoon with milk. Of course my baby still breastfed and had never taken anything from a spoon, so it went everywhere. I was exhausted by it all, but on the way home, I went to the pharmacy and managed to get a pill crusher, and a syringe, so I could give him his medication that way. I had to figure it out by myself; I only mention it because it was the first realisation that from now on there might be a lot for me to figure out, and I would have to be able to do so.

I was a stuck record. I was exhausted, I was terrified, but I remembered and held onto the commitment, and the promise that I had made to my son. That was the important thing. That was the only important thing.

Being a parent is making a commitment to your child and sticking to it.

Twenty-Two: Happy New Year

As 2009 approached, I was getting ready to move back to London after getting the all clear from the hospital. Dr P. had been replaced by Dr. S. who is younger, and looked a bit like George Clooney circa ER. He told me that it's all been a huge mistake, Xavier was fine and there is no doubt about it. Dr. P was just too lopsided at the time. It wasn't his fault. I might have fallen in love with Dr. S, but I couldn't because London was calling. But before that we saw in the New Year with lots of Champagne to celebrate my baby being just fine.

I had never really liked New Year's Eve. I had rarely enjoyed it, although I have had the occasional good one. But unlike Christmas it is definitely not my holiday of choice. I was quite happy to be staying in, I wasn't even planning on drinking because of the breastfeeding, although I did think that when I got the phone call telling me that Xavier was fine I would probably feel like having some bubbles. However, normally, New Year's Eve is pretty much just another day to me.

But it wasn't just another day this year. It was the day when I dreaded and wanted the phone to ring in equal measure. It was the day when I hoped the nightmare would end, or the day I would find out that it would never end. It was a day that if I could have got rid of it, just taken it out of my life, I would. Apparently though it doesn't work like that.

It was the longest day. It was the hardest day. I tried to tell myself that this day all this fear would finally be put to rest but it was getting increasingly hard to believe it.

I was in bed when I got the call from Dr. P. My mother stood by my bed, Xavier was in his Moses basket.

'There's good news and bad news,' he said. I was shaking, I felt sick; I can't even describe the deluge of feelings that fought inside of me.

'The good news is that Xavier has a gallbladder.' Good news? Good fucking news? I didn't even know what a gallbladder was.

'The bad news is that he has Down's Syndrome.' I don't remember what I said to him as I put down the phone. I'm pretty sure I didn't swear though.

My child had Down's Syndrome. How on earth that this happened? I was suddenly a single mother with a Down's Syndrome baby.

When I found out I was pregnant with Xavier my life changed irrevocably. When I gave birth to him, my life changed irrevocably. When I took that phone call my life changed irrevocably. Only this time I really didn't know if I could cope.

As I cried myself to sleep on New Year's Eve, with no idea how I was going to function the following day, or the day after that, or ever again, my last thoughts of 2008 were Down's Syndrome and the fact that I really bloody hated New Year's Eve.

Motherhood: You never know what's round the corner, you just never do.

Twenty-Three: All Fall Down

I look in the mirror and who do I see
I see a girl and she's looking at me
She's young and she's pretty, she's happy and free
Oh how I wish that girl was me

The immediate aftermath of the phone call was a blur. It was like a soft focus photo taken to make you look better than you actually did, but that made everything look far, far worse. I wailed, I cried, I ranted and raved. 'Why me?' I sobbed, then 'why him?' I had approached the end of 2008 celebrating my lovely baby, and I entered 2009 feeling I would never celebrate again.

I fell apart. I remember when I was told my father had passed away I collapsed on the floor. I did get up, but only after I literally fell down. I fell down again, only this time it was figuratively. I didn't know at this point if I would ever get up. And there was this helpless little baby who needed me and I didn't know if I could do it. I didn't know how to get up again.

Often, when something terrible happens, your feelings start doing battle. That's kind of how I saw grief; not just when someone dies, but grief as a part of life. Life is grief isn't it really? You grieve for things that you never had, for things you had but are then lost to you. You grieve for your dreams, your fantasies at times and you grieve the reality. I am not saying this in a maudlin way, just as a fact of life. My life.

As you know I had grieved a lot. In actual fact I should have been really good at it by now. But I wasn't because it's something that doesn't really like you to master it. You are swamped with feelings and emotions that control you rather than vice versa, and sometimes you can't figure out what those feelings are because they all seem to become a mass of confusion. Later, perhaps you can start to untangle the knots that they cause but immediately it is all you can do to keep breathing.

I fed Xavier, I cried. I hugged him so tightly, as if I could make it alright. I asked my mother to take him so I could sleep. I shut down by sleeping; it was my only safe place. I don't remember if I dreamt. Did I reject my baby? Not properly, but I did a bit, yet another thing that I will always have to live with and that I will never forgive myself for. Not only was I drowning in grief but I was also being swallowed up by guilt. I made sure he was taken care of but it was a case of simply going through the motions. Did I stop loving him? I have no idea because I couldn't organise my thoughts at all. I didn't know how I felt, because my emotions were still flinging themselves around in my head and I couldn't catch any of them. For a second I would feel numb, and then I would feel horrendous pain. I cried more than I thought possible. It was a blur but it was also as sharp as a knife. A mass of horrible contradictions and confusion.

I would like, no love, to say that I didn't stop loving Xavier for a minute, and now, looking back, I don't think I did. But I think that that love was buried deep beneath everything else and at the time I didn't have the strength to dig for it. It was there, but it wasn't at the same time.

I looked fabulous. My hair hung limply and even when I mustered the energy to shower and wash it, it looked greasy. I was wearing my huge pyjamas; I felt fatter and frumpier than ever. My eyes were as red as tomatoes and my face swollen from my constant tears. I don't know why my appearance is at all relevant but it was part of the whole, the whole falling down. It was as if the outside of me accurately reflected the inside. I cuddled my sleeping baby. I clutched him tightly to me; as if I let him go I would lose him. Although in some terrible way I felt I already had.

I wished I wasn't alone. I wished that there was someone else for Xavier, a strong someone, who would pick me up and say, 'we can do this for our son.' Although my mother and brother were wonderful, it wasn't the same. I wanted the other person who made him to share this with me, to help me find the answers. But there was only me. I had to be the person with the answers, but I couldn't find her, she was lost.

The worst thing, the very worst thing was that I looked at my son that day, the first day of 2009, and I saw a stranger.

I doubt I will ever forgive myself for that.

The previous day, after the phone call, H, one of my lovely health visitors arrived after my mum called her. At this time I couldn't consider much, let alone how this must have been for my mother. But pain can be very selfish and I had no capacity for myself let alone anyone else. I barely even had capacity for Xavier.

'I'm not dressed,' I sobbed as H hugged me. She took Xavier from me, he woke up. He smiled at her, and she cooed over him.

'I'd be worried if you were dressed,' she said. She didn't tell me that everything would be alright but she said she was there for me. She'd spoken to my GP and he had said there was nothing he could do for me right now, and he was right. Short of changing Xavier's diagnosis, there was nothing anyone could do for me. That was the worst thing, people cared but that didn't matter. It felt like nothing. The cold hard fact was that no one could make me feel better, less afraid; no one could tell me what I wanted, no needed, to hear. I just cried, which is all I seemed to do, and talked, but I could barely remember what I said. But amidst all this, Xavier was bright and alert and smiling.

'It sounds as if he's laughing,' H said, and it really did, as I sobbed some more.

I phoned one of the only people I had confided in about the tests and someone I had already asked to be one of Xavier's Godmothers.

'J,' I sobbed. 'Xavier has Down's syndrome.' Part of me thought by saying it out loud I would feel the reality of that sentence, but I didn't. It was still as if I was watching a film where someone else was delivering the line. There was a shocked silence. Then we talked for a while, and I have no real memory of what was said. I really don't, apart from her saying that she would come and visit me in the next couple of days to see me. She wanted to check that I was alright, whereas we both knew I was far from alright.

Yes, of course I felt sorry for myself. I couldn't believe that this was happening. After everything I had been through, my baby was meant to be the start of the good part of my life. This wasn't supposed to happen. Like a child I wailed and ranted about how unfair everything was.

Throughout this whole horrid ordeal the health professionals were there to support me, but they were clearly also there to check that Xavier was being cared for. Which is exactly how it should be. His wellbeing was the most important thing of course. I believe my maternal instincts were keeping some kind of relationship with my son going, that and my mother's help of course, but it was scary. Almost more terrifying than the diagnosis was trying to be a good mother when I was so, so low. My ability to function was immensely compromised, but somehow I still carried on. Barely, but I did.

One of the ladies that came to visit, said to me that it was clear that I was giving Xavier the love he needed, but I didn't know how I was even doing that. I don't know how I felt, apart from awful, and I don't know how I was going to cope, but everyone seemed certain that I would cope; apart from me that is.

The night after the diagnosis, Xavier screamed as I tried to feed him. This hadn't happened before, and I barely had the energy to cry myself let alone figure out what was wrong with my baby. I cried, he cried, in the end my mum took him from me and I cried myself to sleep. In the morning he was beside me in his Moses basket, all peaceful. But when I tried to feed him, something was wrong. It suddenly occurred to me that he perhaps he wasn't getting enough milk. Xavier had been such a good feeder as I have already boasted. He would also take what he needed and then pull away when he was full. So clearly he was far from full now. My mother phoned the hospital, and they suggested that that I give him formula and at the same time, keep trying to breastfeed.

I notched up another failure to add to my ever growing list; I let my baby go hungry. I did as they suggested and Xavier settled finally. I tried to express milk to stimulate it as I had been told to do but there was less trickling out than usual. I would try for ages and I was so tired, it was horrendous; it was later suggested that my milk dried up due to the shock.

Happy New Year. On the first days of 2009, I was a big fat failure. I had failed to produce a healthy child; I had now failed to feed that child and therefore take care of him properly. The irony wasn't lost on me; I was told by numerous people that Down's Syndrome babies couldn't breastfeed, and Xavier had done but now he had the diagnosis I couldn't feed him. I was a big, fat, failure. And my future, our future looked bleak.

Amidst the despair I had almost forgotten that one of my best friends from university was due to come to visit with her family. She lived in Scarborough which was a bit of a trek to Devon to say the least but was visiting her family in Cheltenham so they had booked into a hotel for the night, just to meet Xavier. I had been so excited about her visit, now I panicked at the thought. I so wasn't ready to face people, even those I adored and I really did adore her. She was one of my favourite people in the whole world.

She had two young girls who I was very close to, and so I had to get up and get dressed and ready to present my baby. I had to try to look as if I wasn't the mad crying woman and even put on make-up. It was all such an effort and I almost didn't make it. I decided that I wasn't going to tell them about the diagnosis, I still hadn't processed it, even remotely, and her two girls would be upset if I was upset and I didn't want that on top of everything else. I thought the only way I could handle the visit was to pretend that everything was fine. I didn't know if I could do it but I did know that I couldn't fall apart, not then.

I still didn't know I would survive it, but I dried my tears, I painted a bright smile on my face and they arrived at our house, armed with gifts. They cooed over Xavier, the girls took turns holding and playing with him, and for a moment I forgot as I saw the joy that I had when I first bought my baby home, before the whole diagnosis nightmare. I saw the joy of a new tiny baby and that was all. I tried so hard to grasp hold of that fact but there was too much else going on in my head and it temporarily slipped from my grasp.

My friend knew about the thyroid diagnosis which seemed bad enough to be honest, because having to medicate your child every single day for the rest of their lives is no small thing in itself. So she knew that it had been stressful, but boy she didn't know the half of it.

I watched the scene as if it was a film scene and not my life. My best friend, her husband and the two adorable girls enjoying my baby. They took turns in holding him and tried to play with him. And you know the worst thing was that for the past few days I hadn't enjoyed Xavier. I had just about cared for him, as you know but I hadn't enjoyed him. I watched them and I saw how it should be, although I wasn't ready to be there yet.

In the evening I decided to have dinner with my friends at their hotel. Mum was happy to look after Xavier. It was so lovely being with my friend and as I was so close to her it felt weird not talking about the very thing that was threatening to destroy me, but at the same time I knew I wasn't ready to tell her or anyone else. We had a lovely dinner and a couple of glasses of wine and it was fun for a while. I think I was able to push the ordeal back a bit, although of course it was there and it threatened to come out. At that dinner I sat with the tears ready and waiting to make an appearance, but luckily I managed, somehow, to hold them in check. But the pleasure of being with friends was something I was almost able to feel. Which should have told me that there was life after this diagnosis, but not quite because I was too busy trying not to cry and fall apart.

I am deeply ashamed of the things I thought in the first few days. It was like the earthquake had happened (measuring very high on the Richter scale) and I was buried in the rubble waiting for the aftershock. I know that a lot of my thoughts and feelings were the result of grief and shock, but nevertheless I am horrendously embarrassed about many things and perhaps will remain so for the rest of my life. However, I need to be honest here. My thoughts were in control of me as were my emotions and there was so much that was irrational happening it was as if I had simply gone mad.

My mother worked for a long period with adults with learning disabilities; I had grown up with that. So why did I react so badly? Was it because before it wasn't my child? Was it just that everything seemed so horrific that I was temporarily a different person. Was I a different person? I didn't know.

I wanted to run away and hide with my baby. Hide him from the world. I thought about moving to somewhere remote, where it would be just the two of us. I would wear long cardigans that were far too big for me and rubber boots all the time, my hair would be wild, I'd look a bit like a mad woman, and no one would be able to hurt us, because no one would be there.

I got a new camera for Christmas, which I had wanted in order to take lots of lovely photos of my beautiful baby and I remember thinking that I wouldn't need it now, why would I take photos? Why wouldn't I take photos? Instead of seeing my beautiful child I saw someone I didn't know; a child with a bowl haircut, a big forehead, wearing brown clothes, special shoes, big tongue. To this day I don't know why I saw that and as I have said, I am deeply, horribly ashamed.

I looked and I saw prejudice, and that prejudice was mine.

I thought about what other people would think. How they would pity me, pity us. I found that unbearable. I imagined those gossips who talked about me when I got pregnant and how they would be saying that it served me right. I thought other people would look down on us, and how they would always feel sorry for me, for Xavier, and that threatened to cut me in half. Perhaps I thought that other people would think these things because I was thinking them, and that was so horrific I was full of self-loathing on top of everything else.

My vulnerability threw up all these thoughts, so I shan't beat myself up too much for them, but I was definitely the most vulnerable I had ever been in my entire life. My baby, as soon as I met him, became the world to me and the fact I couldn't change this for him was excruciatingly painful. I hated feeling like that and I had no idea how to stop it. If I could have taken all my emotions out of me and thrown them away I think I would have done. I could cope with not feeling, with numbness, if it took the pain away. I wanted someone to take my pain away.

I was angry with everyone, especially my father who as you know was no longer with us. I blamed him, I have no idea why. But I thought if he was no longer in this world taking care of us then he should be wherever he was looking after us. I think I just needed someone to blame of course. I had blamed myself, and then I blamed my dead father. There was no logic because logic no longer existed.

Everything felt pointless, from trying to get out of bed in the morning, to getting dressed, to even thinking about the future. What I felt was that my future and my son's future were well and truly over. I felt as if in one phone call that I had lost everything.

I saw unbelievable prejudice and that prejudice was mine.

I saw myself trying on a future that didn't fit me, that didn't fit my child. I was trying to force the wrong piece into the jigsaw but it was never, ever going to go in.

I saw a future that had taken my fantasy and smashed and smashed it until there was nothing left but shards of hurt and pain and I hated it. I hated it. I hated it.

Although I was still in the midst of major confusion, all I knew was that nothing had ever hurt me as much as this and nothing had felt so awful in my life. I couldn't find words to describe the pain but it was physical and I honestly couldn't see how I would ever recover.

But I fed my child and I bathed him. I dressed him and I cuddled him. I replayed the events leading up to this point, from being told I couldn't have children, to being pregnant, to being scared, to being happy. Then I remembered how I said at the time that this baby was meant to be and he was meant to be born to me. So, despite everything the health professionals were right; I did love him more than I have ever loved anyone, and I knew, through my tears and my pain that I would unearth that love again. I couldn't yet, but I knew that I soon would. That was all I knew but for now it was enough.

There are times when being a mother will be the hardest thing you have to do, but somehow you can do it.

Twenty-Four: Five Days

Being a mother means being practical. So I did it, I went on the internet and I found a cure for Down's Syndrome. It took a lot of work to dig it out but there was this new revolutionary treatment that you could get in an Outer Space type clinic in America, by an amazing doctor who looked a bit like Noah Wyle from ER and was just as nice. The treatment was also risk free so I didn't have to worry about it all. It cost an absolute fortune, but I would sell everything I had in order to get it and Xavier would be cured. And therefore so would I.

I tried to remind myself that this condition was happening to Xavier but it felt as if it was happening to me. I went on the internet. I had looked a bit before but retreated because what it told me was too scary. But that was when the diagnosis was an 'if'. Now it was definite, and I thought that I had to confront something, to try to get my head around it somehow; to try to come to terms with it somehow.

It's funny but when I was given the diagnosis no one told me what it meant. As if I should have already known. I didn't know anything about Down's Syndrome apart from the fact that you could see it physically in people (even if so far I had failed to see it in my son). In actual fact I still saw my brother in Xavier when I looked at him. I did suggest that he go get his Chromosomes tested but he said at thirty he probably wouldn't bother. All I knew was that it was described as a disability, a bad thing. Something that could be weaned out before birth if you wanted to. Well, apart from in cases like mine where there was no pre-diagnosis.

It definitely wasn't something that anyone would welcome with open arms but that was all I knew. So with the World Wide Web at my fingertips I decided to find out for myself. Of course, it was far too early for me to do that, and I should have known better. But I thought I was confronting reality head on.

Reality was abhorrent. Here was a condition that threatened to define my son, and therefore define me; to define us.

I was always rubbish at science; I really didn't understand it at all so a lot of what I read went way over my little head. But I managed to glean the simple facts. Down's Syndrome is an extra chromosome (I didn't actually know what a chromosome was). It happens at conception and although the risk increases with the mother's age, more babies with Down's Syndrome are born to younger women. I don't really understand that, but then statistics always make me feel slightly suspicious. They are so often untrustworthy beings. Of course, I was thirty-five when I had Xavier, so straight away there was a way in which I could blame myself for my son's condition. I was too old.

The age debate can rage on but I know many, many women older than me who have had perfectly healthy babies. We have a family friend who gave birth to twins at fifty; they were conceived naturally and they were fine. And the other day on breakfast TV was a nineteen year old who had a child with Down's Syndrome. But at the time, I lacked rationality and so of course I saw it as my fault.

I started to beat myself up; I blamed myself for everything. For every struggle the internet foresaw for my child was my fault. I had done this to him. What kind of mother did that make me? The worst mother in the whole entire world, in fact.

Down's was named after the guy who discovered it and I think it sounds bloody Dickensian. It is also, really depressing and negative. I think it's pretty unfortunate that the bloody guy had to have such a terrible name really. It could have been called Smith or Jones Syndrome, for example, and that wouldn't have been so terrible. The other term for it is Trisomy 21, (after the extra chromosome being number 21) and I won't start ranting here although maybe a name change is in order, but I guess that's a whole other story.

As I read various pages, there in black and white was my child's future. My stereotypical views were largely being supported and upheld. What I read, with an increasingly sinking heart, ranged from all the medical problems that he would be prone to; bad heart, constant colds, digestive problems, weak chest, hearing problems, bad vision; to his learning difficulties, of which there were many; to possible weight problems, to him being unlikely to live independently, to him not being able to have children, (according to one website only three men with the condition have been able to father children); to the high probability of Leukaemia, Dementia and an early mortality. My two month old baby would in all likelihood be dead by the age of sixty five. Just what any mother wants to hear.

Oh and there is no cure. It's just not that kind of thing.

How useful was that? It sent me back to my remote cottage and rubber boots in actual fact. The future looked bleak whichever way I turned.

One of the professionals that came to see me shortly after the diagnosis was trying very hard to be positive and convince me that life would be fine.

'You know there's lots of support out there. He'll learn sign language and we can get him special shoes.' I glared at her. 'And there's a little girl in the village with Down's. She goes to mainstream school. She eats paint but that's OK because we know she does it.'

I sat impassive, but all I wanted to do was to shout and scream. Why does no one stop this girl from eating paint? How do you know my son will need sign language, he's only two months old? I guess she read the same website as me. And as for the special shoes does she not know me at all?

I had quite a stream of visitors in the early days (it still hadn't been a week since the diagnosis). They were all trying to be helpful, but they couldn't be, because nothing they said or did would help. I heard about how amazing Xavier was and although deep down I knew that, I still couldn't see it clearly yet; I was told that it wasn't my fault but I wasn't ready to believe it. One woman even told me that she had had her daughter at forty-one and had been aware of the risks but her daughter was perfectly healthy. Well you couldn't really get much more unhelpful than that. Great! Did she want me to be happy for her? With each visit I would sit there and cry; I was so unable to recognise my life or the life that I wanted, there was little else I could do.

But one visit was more poignant than the others. It was a painfully familiar scene. I was in my pyjamas in bed, because I still didn't have the strength to dress properly most of the time. This lady sat on the bed next to me, she was holding Xavier and I was crying. As there seemed to be so many people checking on me they became a bit interchangeable.

'I just don't know how I can deal with this,' I stated.

'You know you can always have him adopted.' I looked at her, she looked at me. Suddenly, I felt the lioness in me roaring up.

'Are you saying that because my child is soiled goods I can simply give him away? I didn't get the perfect child so I'll get rid and get a better one? Pretend that the pregnancy never happened and the last two months, where I have loved him so, so bloody much never happened? Are you crazy? I'd spend the rest of my life wandering where he was and what he was doing and not seeing him, and oh my God, I feel sick, sick.' I was sobbing and almost shouting at this point.

'So you can deal with this then.' She replied simply, as my baby smiled at her.

I looked at Xavier and thought about never seeing him again, and boy that was the scariest thought that had ever entered my mind. It was scarier than the diagnosis; unbearable in fact. But I still didn't know how I would cope.

Not only had my fantasy been turned on its head before I even got pregnant, now it was standing on its head, then its feet, then its head again. It was doing constant Cartwheels. I thought I had got as far from my dream life as I could already. It turns out I was wrong, wrong, wrong. I was a terrible mother. This was all my fault. I had failed. I'd failed him, I'd failed myself, I'd failed as a mother.

But I hadn't of course. My son, condition or no condition was thriving. He hadn't changed overnight; he was the same baby as he'd been all his short life. He was still beautiful, he was still charming. He was still my little boy. I just couldn't see that clearly yet. I hated myself for it but I couldn't see him, I didn't know where he had gone.

I didn't know what the future held, but then no parent does. I didn't really know what Down's Syndrome meant, but that was something I began to clutch onto. Not only did I not know but I didn't think that anyone did really. They threw up might's and probably's but not many sureties. My son's future wasn't mapped out on that internet site, I was sure of that. I knew very little but I knew that.

I can't tell you exactly when I started to remember who I was. It might have been when I re-read the internet page and thought, instinctively that they were showing me an outdated stereotype, and not my son. Perhaps it was when the lady talked about special shoes. It might have been when I opened my eyes to my own prejudice and felt mortified and ashamed over and over again. It might have been when it was suggested that I give Xavier away. Or when I remembered that this wasn't just about me, it was Xavier who had this condition, and whatever that meant he would have to live with it. Of course because it was about him, it was always going to be about me too, but it was mainly about him.

But I think that it was when I looked at my son, five days after the diagnosis and I thought, 'I know you.' And I did. I might have forgotten for a few days but then I remembered him; he was the same baby I'd carried, and the same baby I had given birth to. The baby I loved and knew so well. The baby who smiled at me and made me melt, the baby I fed and cuddled and sang badly to. The baby whose breath I knew better than my own because I listened to his breathing every single day. The baby who meant the world to me.

Everything had changed, but nothing had changed. Xavier hadn't changed. And I was still his mother. I had a long, long way to go, I knew that but at least I felt as if I had taken that first, difficult step.

Motherhood is not about you; it is about your children, sometimes, often, you need to remember that.

Twenty-Five: Getting up again

Dr. P called me again. He said there had been a terrible mistake. Xavier didn't really have Down's Syndrome, the lab had mixed some results up and they were very sorry to have put me through that. Xavier was fine. He was fine, fine, fine! Then he said he was retiring and would I like to meet the new doctor, Dr. H not because I needed to but because I might like to as he was young, handsome, single and new to the area.

Please don't think from now on this is going to be a book about Down's Syndrome. It's not. What I know about it even now could be written on a postage stamp twice over. This is still my story, the story of me and my baby but suddenly, the uninvited guest, the interloper, Down's syndrome, has gatecrashed said story and is now demanding a part. And I can't throw it out, no matter how much I want to, I can't. The call I believe I might live my life waiting for, like Miss Havisham waiting for her loved one, is never, ever going to come. Damn it.

This is a story about motherhood. Someone said to me that I had to learn in five days what most mothers get five years to learn. I don't know if that is true but Trisomy 21 is integral to this story but it is not the whole story by any means. And of course, I am still searching for my *Happily Ever After.*

Xavier changed. But only in the way that babies change all the time. He smiled a lot, he made little cute noises, he thrived and flourished and grew and was starting to tell me who he was. I know he was only two months old, but every day I was finding something out about him. This is a fascinating time in a baby's life, really, and every day you can discover something new about them if you look. Eventually I looked. I really looked at him.

I changed. Motherhood, parenthood, changes you. I had been in a hole feeling sorry for myself. I was a single mother with a so-called disabled baby. I was dangerously close to becoming a victim of myself. For two months I had been Xavier's mum, and that was all. I still was, of course, but I just had to learn to claw my way out of the hole I was in to get back to that.

I have always seen myself as a fighter. It was other people telling me what my son would/wouldn't do, could/couldn't do that bought out the fighter in me. I finally got up yet again.

I didn't fully get up; I couldn't yet, there was a long way to go. Remember how good I was at denial. Well there was no way that I could go to my usual place this time; I had to go to a different one. Because I knew this was happening and because it was happening to my baby I had to accept it a bit, but there was still huge amounts of disbelief. I couldn't reconcile Xavier, the baby I loved, with the condition that I read about. I wasn't sure I ever would, to be honest. Or if I actually ever needed to. I didn't have much to go on but I kept reading that babies with his condition couldn't breastfeed and I was also told the same thing by health professionals when awaiting the diagnosis. So if they were wrong about that, what else were they wrong about? I clung, tightly onto that. I wasn't sure how much I had to believe, how much I had to accept at this stage, there were so many unanswered questions.

I found it so, so hard to make decisions. But I had to because that's what mothers did. I would get up in the morning and decide what Xavier needed and give it to him. I decided what he would wear; I decided what we would do that day. I decided to give up on breast feeding altogether because my milk was pretty much gone and although I felt guilty about not feeding Xavier myself, I was stressed enough without giving myself extra burdens. So I decided to put Xavier fully on formula.

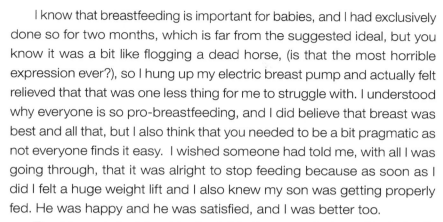

I know that breastfeeding is important for babies, and I had exclusively done so for two months, which is far from the suggested ideal, but you know it was a bit like flogging a dead horse, (is that the most horrible expression ever?), so I hung up my electric breast pump and actually felt relieved that that was one less thing for me to struggle with. I understood why everyone is so pro-breastfeeding, and I did believe that breast was best and all that, but I also think that you needed to be a bit pragmatic as not everyone finds it easy. I wished someone had told me, with all I was going through, that it was alright to stop feeding because as soon as I did I felt a huge weight lift and I also knew my son was getting properly fed. He was happy and he was satisfied, and I was better too.

The biggest decision I took at this time was to keep Xavier's diagnosis largely to myself. My family knew; my family friend and her husband and my friend in Australia. Apart from that and the health care professionals I told no one else. Why? I have no idea; I was acting on instinct. I think it was partly because I still didn't really know how I felt, or how I was going to cope, or what it meant, and also because with everything I was coping with I couldn't cope with pity. I didn't want anyone to pity me and even more pity my son. I couldn't bear the idea that they would feel sorry for us; although I felt sorry for us I didn't want other people to.

I knew that I wasn't ready to talk about this to everyone, and I knew this with a certainty that I hadn't felt about anything since getting the diagnosis.

I knew, deep down that I wanted Xavier to be treated as Xavier and not as a condition; I was also sure about that. Was I ashamed of the condition? Perhaps, but that doesn't make me a very nice person does it? I can't rule it out though. I wasn't ashamed of Xavier, though, I loved him unwaveringly but I still hadn't come to terms with anything.

I decided to keep quiet until the time was right.

In my head, in my imagination, I would never have to tell anyone. Ever. Xavier would just do everything every other child did and no one would notice. I know that Down's Syndrome is a visual condition so I was being utterly deluded but trust me, I needed my fantasy world more than ever now. It had threatened to disintegrate to leave me and I couldn't let it. I think it gave me hope. And more than anything I needed hope.

For a while I became two people. I was Xavier's mother who loved him beyond belief. I was the mother of a baby with Down's Syndrome and I had no idea what that meant. I was far from ready to reconcile the two people, far from ready.

I was tired, so tired but I also needed to don those boxing gloves and fight. The healthcare professionals and Dr P were critical in this. As you know, from his diagnosis, people told me the doom and gloom scenarios. I now know that this will happen throughout Xavier's life. With every appointment I went to, a sentence beginning, 'Down's Syndrome children are more prone/likey to...' would be reeled out within the first few minutes. By the way, I have learnt that there a quite a lot of maybe's in my son's condition and very little certainties. I take comfort in that. But at that time, there was still so much confusion that I really had no idea what the prognosis was. Nor, it seemed, did anyone else.

There was also my old friend instinct. I had little else to trust so I had to trust that. My faithful friend instinct taught me that no one could tell me what would or wouldn't happen to my son, apart from him.

We had to go and visit Dr P. I sat opposite him still resisting the urge to kill him. He asked a number of questions about Xavier. Because I was desperately fighting the diagnosis still, I told him the positive aspects in a slightly boastful way.

'He turns over from his tummy to his back, because he doesn't like being on his tummy.' He did as well, I wasn't making that up.

'Really?' Dr. P said. 'He shouldn't be doing that yet.'

'And you can see how alert he is, he looks around at everything, and he smiles and laughs and he can hold eye contact.' I sounded like one of those annoying pushy mothers you know the type: *Oh yes, Xavier knows his alphabet, can count to twenty and his favourite concerto is Mozart's 6th. Oh I know he's advanced for two months but then he is such a bright baby.*

'He's doing really well,' Dr. P said, encouragingly. I wondered if I should shoot him or drown him in a vat of treacle. Decisions, decisions.

'His condition, there's a scale isn't there?'

'Yes quite a scale, and Xavier seems to be quite mild, dear. Right, well I'll take his blood now.'

Because of Xavier's thyroid problem he had to have his blood taken regularly to check the medication was working. DR. P, took it from his neck. It was the most horrific thing ever as I watched my baby's head held down and then listened to him screaming. It was like something from a horror movie and although I didn't want to be there, I had to be because Xavier needed me. I had to find strength for these little things when I was still trying to find it for the big things. I was so tired but I still tried to keep fighting.

Before we left he asked me if there was anything I wanted to ask him. Of course I did, I wanted to ask what would happen to us? What would our future hold? But he was a doctor, not a fortune teller and I realised then, that he didn't know. The websites might talk about likelihood but that was all, Dr. P. seemed surprised by much of what Xavier did already so what was to say that he couldn't continue to be surprised. He said Xavier was mild, but offered nothing more. So I asked for nothing more. Because I realised at that moment that he didn't know. I didn't know either.

I decided that no one really did, although I suspected Xavier did because he looked so knowing at all times, as if he really did have all the answers, which was a bit annoying really as he was still so tiny and couldn't tell me. But you know sometimes I would look at him and it was as if he was saying 'trust me.' And I realised that I had to do just that. Of course, that could just be me being totally insane, but I really believed it. I really did.

Dr. P. stood up as we made to leave. He awkwardly patted me on the shoulder.

'Well done dear,' he said, and I gave him a look as I resisted the urge to laugh. I carried my baby out of there and I thought I was doing so terribly that for him to say 'well done' was possibly the nicest thing he could have said to me. You see, I wasn't asking for much. And I almost decided not to kill the doctor after all, not even in my imagination.

At later visits with Dr. P. the pattern emerged. He would ask me if I had any questions, I would say no, he would tell me some story or other and tell me how well both myself and Xavier were doing. I always got a pat on the shoulder. One such story involved a lady called Mrs. Tippy something, I seem to remember and a boy with Down's Syndrome.

'For a special treat Mrs. Tippy took a group of teenagers to Pizza Hut, which of course I didn't approve of, but anyway and this lad with Down's went and he ate a whole pizza,' he finished with a flourish.

'I don't get it,' I said.

'Well, you know, it's just like the thing, is that kids will be kids.'

'Oh so Xavier will like pizza when he gets older,' I pushed. I know I can be a major bitch, but hey ho.

'Well, he might do.' Even Dr. P looked confused.

'Good to know,' I said before leaving with my little pat.

Once I called his secretary to rearrange an appointment. She said she would speak to Dr. P and get back to me.

'He said he could fit you in at the end of the day.'

'Yes I don't need long,' I said to her.

'That's what he said, you're always his quickest visit.'

One day after an appointment, I left the hospital and took my baby home I needed to be sure about my new found beliefs. I phoned up the Down Syndrome Association, who were very friendly and helpful.

'I just want to know, what do we actually know, one hundred percent about it?' I asked.

'I guess the best I can tell you is that we bred some mice with Down's and that concluded that they could do what other mice could do only it took them longer.'

So the Down's mice could do what the other mice could do then my son could do whatever anyone else did. If it took him longer then that wasn't the end of the world. What I discovered from that phone call was to expect a developmental delay of some sort. Which didn't tell me much, and that gave me hope. All children, conditions or not, develop

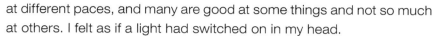

at different paces, and many are good at some things and not so much at others. I felt as if a light had switched on in my head.

I had learnt something new. I had learnt something so incredibly crucial. No one did know what the future held and therefore I didn't need to listen to the crap. I could ignore them all; I didn't have to listen to the maybes.

I decided I would only listen to two voices from now one. My son's voice and my instinctive voice. The only two voices I could trust.

Being a mother means listening to your child from the moment they are born.

Twenty-Six: I am just a mother

I wouldn't move to London, not yet anyway. I would stay in Devon where I felt safe. Near my family. Near the sea. And it wasn't all bad. Xavier and I would get our own little home and his room would be gorgeous and we would spend the summer on the beach. We would probably get talking to a number of gorgeous surfers and eventually I would fall in love with a surfer who also happened to be a very successful business man, and who loved children. He'd be a bit weather beaten but in a sexy way not in an alcoholic-who-lives-on-the-street kind of way. I just had to lose a bit more weight before I got into a swimsuit let alone a wetsuit.

Are wetsuits the most unflattering item of clothing ever? I know they are practical but I have a real problem with stuff that you wear being practical. But there I was thinking of designing a wetsuit that didn't hug you so intimately when it was pointed out that then it wouldn't keep you warm. I was incredibly annoyed about that, as I was planning on making my fortune with it. I really liked the idea of surfing but I would have to lose a lot of weight before I went anywhere near a wetsuit, I can tell you.

My grieving process wasn't anywhere near complete and I wondered if it ever would be. I did have to face the fact that this grief might be part of my life forever. And forever seemed like a very long time. The tears were still a constant, as was the panic and the fear, and the immense pain that I felt on waking and through most of the day. Despite making progress it was still a whole terrifying mess. I still hadn't come to terms with everything but I had come to terms with one thing. That I wouldn't be moving home to London anytime soon. I hadn't yet ruled out moving back, forever, but I wanted to put it on hold until my life was back on track, or at least I was back on track. I wasn't sure if that would ever happen at this stage, but I knew I had to be at home for now. More than anything else, I really needed my mummy. On a practical level, on an emotional level, on so many levels I was where I needed to be. For now at least.

My London friends asked me when I would be coming home.

'Probably not for a while, Xavier and I are still finding our feet and I really need my mum around.'

'But we miss you.'

'I know and I miss you but being here is best for Xavier right now.'

'What about you?'

'What's best for him is best for me. Honestly, it's not forever.'

'It better not be. I don't want you wearing velour and bad shoes just because you live in Devon. And make sure you straighten your hair, especially the back.'

'Of course,' I promised and then went to unearth my hair straighteners and throw my velour jogging pants away.

A few of my friends bless them, did seem to think that you required a passport to even visit Devon, and that no one here knew how to dress. I forgave them their prejudice; they didn't get out of the city much.

I hadn't forgotten myself but again it went back to the fact that I had to do what was best for Xavier because that was best for me. And actually the idea of living in the big city, having to deal with the health professionals, doctors and so on that I didn't know filled me with dread. I could barely deal with the ones that I knew and on the whole they were pretty good, despite my complaints. I had a good support system at the moment even if I didn't actually like what anyone said to me, and I think I would have been ever so slightly crazy to give that up.

And London isn't cheap. Xavier and I would have to live in a tiny flat if we were lucky. I would never go out because I wouldn't be able to afford a babysitter. Oh, and I would miss my family, of course. No, I knew where I needed to be.

I was scared enough without taking another leap into the unknown. Because it was unknown. London might have been my home for years and years but with Xavier, with all this, it wasn't somewhere I knew. Again, instinctively I knew the right thing was to stay here. But still I only meant temporarily.

I sometimes wondered if there is a cruelty to fate that was playing with me. I remember at eighteen being desperate to leave Devon to move to the city (I went to Bristol to university), and saying that I would never live here again. I think my words might have been along the lines of:

'I shall never live in this Godforsaken place ever again.' Which I deeply regret now, obviously.

I still hadn't planned on living in North Devon forever, but here I was, and actually although I could barely admit it to my teenage self, I was actually seeing its attraction. Beautiful countryside, sandy beaches, rain, wind... On the whole, it was actually a pretty good place to live. I could certainly see that it was a wonderful place to bring up a child. My teenage self would be absolutely horrified with me.

I saw it though, at this stage, as merely a practical decision. You see I wasn't sure emotionally where I was let alone where I wanted to be. I was still terrified, I felt as if someone was chasing me with a knife on a daily basis but I knew that wherever I was, I needed to start getting myself out and back into real society. Real Devon society.

But I still didn't know anyone. I didn't want to go back to the breast-feeding group, despite liking a couple of people there. I was scared of going, and I felt ashamed of myself still. I had no confidence and I felt I was wearing my vulnerability like a dress. Also, (and probably most importantly), I was no longer breastfeeding. As one of the volunteers was still breastfeeding her four year old I kind of thought that if I bought out a bottle of formula they might lynch me. Imagine that in the local paper *'New mum gets beaten to death with a nappy for bottle feeding her child.'*

I tried going out into the local town but my awkwardness seemed to grow when outside my house. I remember pushing Xavier around and literally counting healthy children. It was pretty sick actually. I was still resisting victimhood but 'why him?' still reverberated round my head along with 'why me?' I was also looking at mothers and wondering what they had done to deserve a healthy condition free child, which I know is awful. The thing is I didn't want to swap my child, I loved him far too much for that, I wanted Xavier, but Xavier without this condition. That was what I wanted and that was what I couldn't have.

I found even simple things difficult. I would go to *Blockbusters,* to try to get something to watch but the films depressed me. I felt like having a fully fledged tantrum in the shop as I looked at the comedies with disgust. It was as if I didn't want to laugh, although I desperately did. Everywhere I went I saw contradictions. Everywhere I went I felt as if I was in a foreign country.

I still took Xavier to the clinic on a weekly basis to get him weighed and although there were lots of healthy babies there I coped because the health visitors were there for me. They would still usually make me a coffee and a chat and it was then that my health visitor told me she was referring me to a course they ran for new mothers. It was called *'Here's looking at you baby.'*

'What is it?' I asked, without the energy to be interested.

'It's a ten week course about getting to know your baby, and their emotional needs and that sort of thing. It's really popular but I will try to get you on.'

'It sounds like something for mums that are struggling,' I said. I was struggling but I didn't want to be seen as such. Also, because I felt of myself as a failure I wasn't sure if I could be strong enough to go to such a group.

'Not at all. It's for everyone and seriously most people who go, say they found it valuable.' I didn't believe her but I needed to do something before I drowned in loneliness. She told me a little more and actually I thought that it would be good for us both. For Xavier to meet other babies, and me to meet other mothers. To actually have to get dressed and leave the house. I soon came round to the idea.

When you feel low just leaving the house can seem daunting. I had been out since the diagnosis but I hadn't found it easy and then it was just me and Xavier. Now, I was going out to a social environment and although I needed and actually wanted to go I was still incredibly anxious.

I felt as if I was wearing some kind of sign saying I was a terrible mother, that I would be judged, that my son would be treated differently, I didn't know exactly, but it was scary and part of me wished I never had to go out ever again. I still thought about my remote cottage with wonky walls. But I needed to get Xavier and me a life, so I straightened my hair (even the back), put on some make up, packed up all I might need for my baby and off I went. I looked in the mirror and despite being heavier than I would have liked, I looked more like myself than I had in a while. I just still wasn't sure I felt it.

I arrived at the first session purposefully early. I went up to I, the lady running the course and introduced myself.

'I know my health visitor told you about Xavier but I don't want to tell anyone else,' I said, slightly defensively. Which was how I felt at the time. I was beginning to think that I had to brace myself to fight with everyone which was sad.

'Why would you? He's just a beautiful baby and you're his mother.'

I fell in love with her, then and there. She is truly one of the people I credit with helping me get my strength back. She was so non-plussed by the diagnosis that it almost seemed as if she shrugged her shoulders; 'so what?' she seemed to be saying. And that was where I wanted to be. And knowing that I wanted to be there gave me something to aim for.

The course was lovely; my health visitor was right. I wished it could have been available to every mother. It showed us that babies were amazing from a very young age and how you could get to know them and their emotions from the day they were born. It's funny but I have heard a number of people say that babies are boring, which I don't understand at all. I found my baby so fascinating and perhaps everyone who thinks otherwise should go to *Here's Looking at you Baby*. I learnt a lot and I felt secure in that room. That was huge for someone who believed she would never feel secure again.

As the session began we all traipsed in with our babies and they would make us coffee and tea and even biscuits. As I was no longer breastfeeding I had weaned myself back onto caffeine. Boy that felt good. The rest of the group seemed nice; E from the breastfeeding group was there and it was good to see her. There were six other mothers and a father in the group. I made friends with some of them that I still see to this day. This was nothing like Parentcraft, as everyone was really friendly, and it was smaller and more intimate than the breastfeeding group. The babies were all lovely and each had their own characters as did the parents. It was funny but what we learnt was that all babies are individuals who like different things from birth. That really struck a chord with me.

Xavier might have Trisomy 21, or Down's Syndrome or whatever you want to call it, but he was an individual, as different from the babies in that room who didn't have his condition as he would be from the babies who did have his condition. I put that in my pocket and promised never to let that go.

Finally I felt as if I could do it, I could stay here and make friends and Xavier and I would have a life. My remote cottage began to get more remote.

It was funny as well, Xavier was one of the youngest there and the course was held when he normally napped, so we would sit around in a circle, my baby nestled into me, and Xavier became known as the sleeper. When he slept on my chest, tucked into my neck, someone commented on how lucky I was that he liked to sleep that way and how their baby wouldn't settle like that on them.

'He really fits you,' she said. And he did. Like a jigsaw piece he fit me and I fit him.

Normally before the end he would wake up, I would give him some milk and then he would notice the other babies. One session he was laid on the floor, on his back in between two baby girls. He kept turning to one and then the other, smiling as if he couldn't make up his mind which one to pay attention to.

'He's flirting,' one of the mothers said, and it looked as if he was. He would make all these noises, as if he was talking, and he would turn around to ensure he could look at everything. I was just another mother, and Xavier was another baby and I cannot tell you how priceless that feeling was.

Just as each baby in the room was different, all the parents were too. There were some mums who were so immaculate that I could only envy them. They were also really slim. There was one mum who seemed less relaxed than the others and worried about her baby constantly. The father in the group was really into development and would harp on about that a lot, being a bit to scientific for me. I was a talker and I talked too much, probably a result of my loneliness, I guess. Another mum had three other children so she seemed like a pro who took everything in her stride. I was just a mother, although there is no 'just' about motherhood.

Because the course taught us about our babies, or it taught us how to learn about our babies, I felt my bond with Xavier strengthen.

After the first *Here's Looking at You Baby*, session, my new favourite person, I, came to visit me to do something called a Brazelton assessment. Named after pediatrician, T. Brazelton, it evaluates a baby's behavior to build a profile of babies in the first couple of months of their lives. I won't go into details, but it's interesting for new mothers to look into it, as it checks various responses. The aim was for the parent to be able to use the results to help in the building of their relationship because Brazelton recognises that a baby is highly developed even when newborn. For me though it was also imperative in showing how well Xavier was doing, how responsive he was and how strong. Whatever the test was and I am not going into the details here, it felt as if Xavier passed (although apparently it wasn't that kind of test) and when I left I felt even more reassured that my baby was who I thought he was. I could never thank her enough for that.

You see one of the things that I had was doubt. Buckets full of doubt. Remember how I said I couldn't reconcile my baby to the internet sites I read, well that was because he wasn't what I read, he was who he was. There was so much I didn't know about him, of course as he was only a few months old, but there was a lot I did. I just had to trust myself, to trust my instincts. It was back to that old chestnut.

Xavier was beautiful, he was clever, he was alert, he was charming and he was my baby. And I was so, so lucky to be his mummy.

Around that time I phoned J, my family friend, and I said that I knew now I hadn't failed because I couldn't look at Xavier, my beautiful little boy, and see him as any kind of failure, and that was my major turning point.

A Mother should see their children as perfect because all children are.

Twenty-Seven: Motherhood in heels

In the sequel to my bestselling book, 'How to be the best at being pregnant,' 'How to be the best at being a mum,' I talk in length about how one of the most important aspects of motherhood is maintaining a balance between being a mother and being an individual. It's not easy to achieve this, I acknowledge that; but you can do it. You can also look super stylish at the same time. How to do this and the other priceless advice I give in the book, goes some way to explaining how I won the best mother ever award.

I have already said that motherhood changes a person. It's inevitable and there is no way you can stop it. Nor should you want to. Being a mother becomes a huge part of who you are. However, it doesn't necessarily become the whole you. Your identity changes but at the same time being a mum shouldn't be your whole identity. I think for new mothers, it probably does, for a while. And in my case, well first there was the single mother thing, and then there was the whole diagnosis, so my identity was heaving under the weight of everything that was going on. I didn't stop and think about who I was then because I didn't have the time, or the energy. But I was definitely lost and part of what I had lost was my identity.

Again, I am not trying to make you all feel sorry for me, (well, I might be a bit), but I had undergone so many changes that it was inevitable that there were going to be casualties and my identity might have been one. I am not saying that it was gone forever but like Hansel and Gretel, I had shed bits of it whilst on my journey for me to trace and get back later. There was a whole trail of Faith somewhere, I was just not ready, or able to go back and pick it up. I had left London, my friends, I'd had my baby, I'd been lonely, I'd had the awful diagnosis and had only just started going out again, and I was still largely wearing fat or elasticated clothes. With all of this, I actually had little idea who I was anymore.

But a step toward finding myself was to go and see my friends; it was time for us for take our first visit to London. I had planned on going in the New Year, but that turned out not to be such a good time. I missed my friends terribly and only Charlie had met Xavier. So I decided to take a kind of holiday, for nearly two weeks to stay with a couple of friends and let them meet my baby. I dusted off my high heels, dug out clothes which weren't too elasticated, and booked a train ticket. I think it was definitely a step in the right direction, although I was quite simply terrified.

I had never travelled with Xavier before, and although he was only three months old and quite small he still needed a lot of stuff. He was on formula and although of course there were shops in London, I needed stuff to last me the first few days. There were bottles and bibs, and nappies and formula and all his medication and baby wipes, nappy sacks, the list went on and on. I also, seemed to think that Xavier needed a different outfit every day, which meant that when I packed there was a huge suitcase full of things, mainly for my baby, and I could barely lift it.

I managed to sneak in a pair of heels for me as well and my hair straighteners. We were ready for our first official visit to London town.

We settled on the train and Xavier immediately proved himself to be a good traveler. He barely murmured the entire journey and I felt excited, and I couldn't remember the last time I had felt that. But I kept telling myself over and over again that I was just Xavier's mother and we were going to see my lovely girls. As the train drew into Paddington station I felt that pang that I normally got whenever I returned to London; I felt as if I was going home.

I had debated long and hard about whether or not to tell them about Xavier's diagnosis. These were friends who knew nearly everything about me. They hadn't seen me this time but they had seen me through my other tough times and I loved and trusted them implicitly. And fleetingly I wondered if they would be angry with me for keeping it from them, but I immediately realised that that wasn't my primary concern. I wanted them to meet Xavier as Xavier and not the condition that I was going to fight hard not to let define him. I fleetingly wondered if people would guess but then if they did that wasn't my primary concern either. My primary concern was for people to meet Xavier and know him for who he was, and not have any preconceptions of who he was. After all that was what I was fighting hard to do myself. I was still finding my way and I simply wasn't ready to talk about it.

I have always been contradictory when it came to talking about myself. One minute I'd be wearing my heart on my sleeve, other times I'd clamp up until I could sort things out in my own head. Put simply I still didn't know how I was feeling about the diagnosis or even how I was going to cope with it. Instinctively I knew at this point in time I didn't want to talk about it; I wasn't anywhere near ready.

I worried that I shouldn't expect too much of people. After all, look at the way I had reacted. I wanted Xavier treated as an individual, and I was simultaneously petrified that he never would be. I worried that now Xavier had been stamped and branded and labeled by others, that label would be the first thing they saw, or the only thing they saw. If my preconceptions became their preconceptions and what if people couldn't get past that the way I had? That was what truly terrified me.

Again, I looked to my instincts and they told me to keep stum; I did.

I immediately shed the skin of sadness as I arrived. I knew that there was a lot for me to deal with but I suddenly remembered who I was. I had a purpose and that purpose was to see my friends and introduce my gorgeous son to them. I just had to focus on doing that. And I was going to do it in heels.

Charlie met me at the station.

'Hi darling. God, do you really need all that?' She blanched as she lifted the suitcase. I kissed her cheek.

'Of course I do, you know I was never any good at travelling light.' Xavier was asleep in his pram as we made our way to the taxi rank. It was his first journey in a black cab and he slept all the way through it. We arrived at our first port of call, my friend, H, who had a little girl just over a year older than Xavier. I hadn't seen them for ages but immediately amidst the tea and hugs, it was as if we had never been away.

As we settled in, it became strange being away from Devon. I was happy to be in London but ever so slightly anxious, as if I was out of my comfort zone, which I was. There was no mum to call on every five minutes and also, although we were staying with really lovely friends, nothing was as familiar as it was at home. But we managed. My friend had a nanny who commented that she had never met a baby as young as Xavier who was so alert. I took pride in that. And I realised, as I showed my baby off, that I was so proud of Xavier. I presented him to my friends with a huge flourish. My gorgeous little boy. And that was exactly how he was received.

I took Xavier shopping on the Kings Road, which was one of my favourite shopping streets in London, and I bought things for both of us that I couldn't get in North Devon. I am not going to put down my new home, but for shopping it was definitely no great shakes. There were two things I missed about London; shopping and friends. Oh and Sushi. Actually, thinking about it there was quite a lot but don't get me started.

One night, my friend's husband babysat and we went out to dinner and to see a film. It was great, one of my only evenings out since Xavier was born. We had dinner in a French restaurant with wine (boy get me, the grown up) before going to the cinema. I did nearly get thrown out of the restaurant for asking for ketchup with my fries but then, I don't get out much and I apologised profusely to the lovely French waiter who tutted indignantly at me. My whole social life in Devon was restricted to baby groups, going out for the evening was such a treat. Oh my goodness, I almost felt like an adult.

However, what I didn't miss was the transport. I had a chauffeur at home (my mother), and in London with Xavier and his massive pram I had to get taxis everywhere. And London taxis aren't cheap, so I spent the equivalent of Xavier's first year of school fees on getting around. That was the only down side.

After a few days I went to stay with another friend who had a little boy of four. He introduced Xavier to anyone he met as his brother, which was so incredibly cute. Although of course that meant everyone thought I was the mother of both boys, and I didn't really think it would do any good for me to explain. So when they said, 'you must have your hands full,' I laughed and nodded. Then felt like an idiot. But never mind. We were in Primrose Hill and I would wheel him around the park in his pram to get him to sleep, and look out over London, (my favourite view of London is from the top of Primrose Hill), wondering if I would ever live there again.

Because what became clear was that it was no way as easy as living in Devon. Getting around was so much harder, sometimes it felt impossible. There was no way I could negotiate escalators on the tube or fit my pram on the crowded buses. I know most mothers would have used those sling things, and I guess I would if I had lived in London but I wasn't too keen at the idea of them. I always thought they suited men much more than women and I didn't have a man either. I would have hired a cute manny but I couldn't afford it. Anyway, I thought that if I did manage to get a small flat, I wouldn't be able to leave it much because it was just too damn hard. Not until Xavier was walking and we could take the tube or the bus anyway. On a practical level, London didn't work for me and Xavier; that rapidly became depressingly clear.

To cheer myself up, we went to lunch at *Soho House* with three of my best girlfriends. Clever Xavier was asleep as we toasted him with Champagne and ordered lunch, and he slept the whole way through it. When he woke I got him ready for a feed.

'How do you feed him? Is your wet nurse waiting outside?' my friend T asked.

'Yes, I told her to stand there until I called her,' I replied as I whipped out my bottle and some formula. T was most disappointed.

'He looks very wise, you know, but he doesn't look as formidable as he did in the photos, I was a bit scared of him at first but I'm not now,' she finished.

'Xavier is going to love his Auntie T as he gets older.'

As we whiled away the afternoon there, Xavier attracted a lot of attention.

'Lots of guys seem to be cooing over Xavier,' one friend said.

'Great, I can use my child as bait then,' I replied, not really seriously. I hope.

Xavier loved being there. He looked around at everything, as he always does, and he smiled a lot. One of the things I had learned about my son already was that he liked being out, he liked having lots of different things to look at. I was very hopeful that he would take after his mother and like dining out a lot, because that would be very handy.

After an incredibly long lunch, we went home, and I put Xavier to bed, telling him he was extra clever. And although his mummy was tipsy she was managing pretty well, mothering in heels.

The two weeks had reminded me how much I loved my friends, it reminded me of who I used to be and who I still was to an extent. I saw my son through their eyes and that was pretty special too. The whole visit was positive on the whole and I was so glad I had stepped out of that comfort zone to do it.

When I bid farewell to London it was with mixed feelings. I wanted to get home because I missed the ease of life, but I wished my friends were all there. I had shown Xavier to people who I hoped would be part of his life forever and would love him. I had found a bit more of my identity, and now I felt confident that I would find more. I wasn't sure when or where but now I knew I would.

Motherhood is always a bit about finding yourself at the same time as finding out who your child is.

Twenty-Eight: There's no such thing as normal

I will never give up on my fantasies but they aren't quite so prominent in my life at this moment in time. Perhaps I am scared of them, perhaps I think that as reality has produced something so opposite from my dreams I should stop dreaming. Or perhaps reality has edged into my fantasies a bit too much spoiling them for me. At each stage in this part of my life I had to grieve for the future I'd planned and readjust my visions. My expectations and hopes will never be lowered, though, just like my fears will never go away. However, I will always see a perfect life for us, and I will always strive for it. I will always have my fantasies; I will never give up on them.

In the early days after Xavier's diagnosis I wrote in my diary that 'for two months I was a normal mother but I will never know what it's like to be a normal mother again.' I was a bit of a drama queen, although perhaps that was warranted. I would always fight with the dichotomy of Xavier's condition. He was becoming such a person that he was just Xavier but then with all the appointments we had to go to and people we had to see I could never fully forget. But then I was a mother and all mothers were different as all children were, so it was a pretty stupid thing to say as there really was no such thing as normal.

I had taken little steps toward getting my head around what was happening to us. I still believed I never fully would, but there was a glaring reality facing me, and although I still didn't exactly know what that reality was, I was starting to take control again. I knew I had done this because I had acknowledged that I would never be able to be in control. At various times throughout my life when I felt out of control, I took whatever I could control and ran with that.

I believe, strongly, that whenever a major change happens in your life you need a period of catching up with said change. You can't accept it straight away, you often don't welcome it. There is a period playing of catch up. I had this with every major change; losing my father, losing my relationship, my career problems. I often found myself playing catch up, but then that made me remember that in the end you do catch up. I always caught up, in fact, even if it took me a long time.

No mother, no parent, can ever fully control their lives once a child enters it. It just doesn't happen. If someone sat me down before I gave birth and asked me what kind of child I wanted, I would say; a baby who is healthy, a baby who sleeps, one who rarely cries but always smiles, a gorgeous baby, a clever baby, a baby who is just divine. Then if they asked me what kind of child I would like that baby to grow up to be, I would say; a healthy child, a spirited child, a confident child, a bright child, a popular child, a child who smiles, a child who is just divine. And on it would go until we reached what kind of adult would I want my baby to become and I would say; a healthy adult, a successful adult, a happy adult, an adult who is loved and who has his own, wonderful family…

When I thought about this, and thinking about it was triggered by I, from *Here's Looking at You Baby*, and also my trip to London, I realised I pretty much got the baby I asked for. Apart from his diagnosis which I can't even say resulted in me thinking of him as unhealthy because Xavier was pretty healthy. I don't know what kind of child exactly Xavier would be but he definitely seemed spirited, and he would smile a lot because he always did, and I also believed he was bright and I was prepared to argue that point. I didn't mean necessarily that he would be a genius or even academically clever, but I knew Xavier had an intrinsic intelligence, I just knew it. But from getting to know Xavier as a person because that's what all babies were, I knew that from a young age he knew what he liked and didn't like. He didn't like being on his tummy, he liked lying on his back, for example, and he told me, showed me. So I was pretty sure that he would continue in this vein. The rest, the future I had to let go off because like any parent, much of it is out of your hands.

What I did have some control over was the present. I needed to forge a future for me and my son and the only way I could do that was to start sorting out the present. I had so many voices in my ear, as I have said, that I largely stopped listening to them. Call my crazy but I started to look for anyway I could to help Xavier and therefore help me.

I took him to the Cranial Osteopath. I knew very little about it, but I had read that it helped with strengthening the head, making it easier for babies to hold their heads up and other good things. And let's face it there's not a huge amount of alternative therapies that you can take your baby to. And I wasn't quite crazy enough to take Xavier to a Faith healer, or a Witch doctor, throwing money at them to get him a cure. Well, actually I might have done but you really don't find many Witch doctors in North Devon.

The Cranial Osteopath explained that they could often help babies who had colic, or constipation or were bad sleepers or were grumpy. She probably told me more than that but that was what I took in. None of that really applied to Xavier but she said she worked with babies a lot and could ensure that he was balanced and help strengthen his head. He wasn't a particularly floppy baby, but as I said, anything I could do I would do.

L, Xavier's cranial Osteopath was lovely. I sometimes believe it was fate that we met. As I explained that I didn't trust what people told me about Xavier's diagnosis and how my desperate wish was to keep him from being labeled, she looked at me.

'I have Cerebral Palsy, and I'm fine.' I smiled at her and I felt so much relief, so much vindication. I know it was different but the same principal. A person doesn't have to become their diagnosis. And she had a career she loved, which in my book meant her condition hadn't exactly held her back. Not at all.

I watched as she held Xavier's head, and I have no idea what she was doing, or even if she was doing anything, but after a few sessions, Xavier was holding his head up pretty well and we applauded his strength. He might have done so anyway but you never quite know that. It's another leap of faith, but it made me feel as if I was doing something positive. I needed to feel that I was taking action to help my child, doing everything I could, and this helped me feel that way. It wasn't exactly cheap but I felt that it was worth it for the peace of mind that it gave me and it also made me feel that I was being proactive. A good mother. At the time I took Xavier once a week and it made me feel a little less useless.

I went on a diet. If I was going to get our lives back on track that was something I needed to do. I was no longer breastfeeding so I couldn't justify the eating anymore. And also I was pretty fed up with wearing maternity or fat clothes. As much as I loved my elasticated pants, it was time to get rid of them. It wasn't easy, trust me but it was time. I joined the gym, and I actually went.

Of course my idea of dieting wasn't that straight forward. I decided that what I was going to do was to only eat once a day. This worked for a friend of mine who said that you can drink as much coffee with skimmed milk as you want to fill you up and then have a pretty good dinner. Her theory was that way you could pretty much eat what you wanted, just only once a day. For some reason I quite liked the sound of that, so I tried it. It wasn't easy and of course I knew it wasn't healthy. Just to be clear I am definitely not recommending this diet after all, I was hardly at my sanest was I? But anyway, with exercise and my slightly unhealthy diet, the weight finally started coming off.

Also, I have another friend who only eats every other day. But she has a three course meal every other day which is nice right? I am not criticising or promoting any of these diets, but I didn't have time for Weight Watchers, although I did toy with the idea of doing it, and I didn't like the Atkins, so this was my diet of choice.

I also met a mum locally who ran an old fashioned aerobics class in the village hall. That was pretty good actually even if it did remind me just how uncoordinated I was. When I was at University someone persuaded me to go to a Step class. Somehow I ended up getting my foot tangled in a five aside football goal net and I fell over and it stopped the class, so of course I never went back again. Nothing that bad happened but I still didn't seem to be able to get my arms and legs to work at the same time.

Some people told me that one of the characteristics of Xavier's condition would be a lack of co-ordination; well with a mother like me the poor kid stood no chance.

My friend who I did tell about Xavier; my Australian friend, and who I had actually seen back in London and I talked a lot. One of my aims of keeping it quiet was that I didn't talk about the diagnosis all the time, and actually let it define me as it threatened. Because that was another dichotomy I faced. I wanted to talk about it but I didn't want to talk about it all the time. I was scared I would talk about nothing else if everyone knew; I was worried that it would be all I talked about.

There was a freedom from it which I would, in time, learn to enjoy when everyone knew, but that wouldn't happen overnight.

'You know hon, I've given it a lot of thought, and I believe that this whole thing is a load of rubbish. What if I treat Xavier as if he's normal, and give him extra help but not treat him as if he's disabled, how do we know that that won't work?'

'We don't. No one does. I know of someone with Down's who is an accountant.'

'I'm not sure I want Xavier to be an account,' I joked. 'I'm kind of talking about how I treat him. I'm not saying that he won't have any problems but I believe we can overcome nearly everything. That's what I've always done in some way isn't it? If I just accept it and think that Xavier is going to have loads of problems, then he will won't he? But if I expect things to be fine and just give him extra help where it's needed then what's to say that that won't give him the best chance in life. It's nurture over nature.'

'That's a good point. And you know most children have things they struggle with. I couldn't tie my shoe laces until I was thirteen.'

'You probably shouldn't tell people that. It's part of him, I accept that but it's not everything. And you know I'm a fighter, that's what I do, and I'm prepared to fight this. Also, thinking about it, he is still his mother's son.'

'You know, you're right, he has your DNA. People forget that, don't they?' And it was true. Xavier might have lots of things in him but he had part of me and I would bet money he had the good bits.

I know I have to be careful what I say about Xavier's father but when I was pregnant I used to say to friends; 'I hope that he gets his father's height and my brains. If it's the other way round he'd be screwed.' I am only 5ft 2. Anyway, that was what I thought then and what I think now is that he might have extra challenges to face but if he's got my fighting spirit that won't daunt him. Like his mother he will always have his boxing gloves handy. I just really hoped, and prayed that he didn't have to use them too much. I certainly hoped he wouldn't need them as much as I had done.

It's hard because I kept remembering the commitment I made to my child. All parents want the best for their children. You want them to be healthy and happy, and popular and successful. You want them to have options in life, to be able to make choices that suit them. You want to give your child everything. I wanted so much for Xavier and I refused to let that go. I had hold of it and I wouldn't let go, nor would I let anyone prise my fingers off of it. But I also had to remember that no matter what I wanted for Xavier what would be more important would be what Xavier wanted for himself. That was what I really needed to hold onto.

Following our conversation, my friend found an article on the internet and for once it was interesting and positive. Basically it said that if you were told your baby was going to be extra bright you would stimulate them and work with them to encourage that. So if you're told you're baby isn't going to be bright or physical do you just leave them to lie in the cot without stimulation? This woman had a baby with Down's Syndrome and she shared exactly the attitude that I was developing. People were constantly surprised by her child, and one even said; 'I thought she was supposed to be retarded.' Horrible, but that happened.

Suddenly I didn't feel as if I was insane. I clearly wasn't the only person who thought this way. I could do this and I would do this. And if I was mad then at least I wasn't the only mad one.

For two months I had stimulated Xavier before his diagnosis and I continued to do so. I wasn't going to stop or treat him as if there was anything wrong with him. Because there wasn't. Even with this condition that didn't mean that it was wrong. We are all different, my friend reminded me of that. I can write books but struggle with telling my left from my right, and I have absolutely no sense of direction. She only recently could wear lace up shoes, and probably at an age when she didn't even want to anymore. But we didn't let that hinder us unnecessarily. Well apart from the fact that I get lost. A lot.

I found a website for a place called 'Brainwave' for children with any kind of condition. I spoke to someone there. They didn't take babies until they were six months old but what I liked was that they treated children as individuals not as a condition and they evaluated them as such, helping in areas where they needed help. What they said was that they focused on what children could do not what they couldn't do. It sounded just what I was looking for. I booked Xavier in for almost the minute he was old enough.

It was a charity and subsidised but you had to pay a bit. I didn't have much money but I was determined and my mum started looking for available help and grants to apply for. However, it just made me feel there was some more control in this after all, and that was what I was looking for. I was tired of listening to the gloom merchants, and although I had lots of people around us that either shared my attitude or were beginning to, I still wanted more positivity. I wanted to be surrounded by it, and it also went back to the commitment I wrote to my son; I promised him and I would keep that promise.

I was aware that there was a danger of me pushing too hard. A danger that I would be so determined that Xavier didn't fall to behind that I would push and push him. What if I tried to make him *superchild* and in doing so forget to let him be who he was? But then I remembered that the only reason I had come to this conclusion in the first place was because I knew my child pretty well and would continue to do so. I would only act on his cues. And that is what any parent should do. I knew that Xavier would tell me or show me what he was and wasn't capable of, and I would help with anything, in just in case he needed it.

'*Here's Looking at you Baby,*' finished, and we started going to other toddler groups. I also booked Xavier some swimming lessons, and started to arrange play dates (which were really coffee dates in disguise). Our social life was getting pretty full and Xavier flourished. He loved swimming; he giggled and smiled in the water seeming confident and at home there. I wondered if that was because he was born in the water because he didn't mind even when I dunked him.

The lessons we went to involved dunking our babies under the water and the first time I had to do it I felt so guilty, but Xavier didn't seem to mind. The swimming lessons were pretty awful for me but Xavier loved them. In fact he was far more confident in the water than his mummy was. I tended to do my best to keep my head above the water, and not just in the swimming pool.

Each time I went to a new group I would feel butterflies in my tummy and slightly vulnerable still, but I would take a deep breath and try to find my confidence. I knew there was some left, but it was playing a game of hide and seek with me. And each time it got slightly easier. I made more friends, and felt like a mother. A proper mother. No, actually *Supermum*. That was what I was striving for. I had to know that I was the best mum I could be; the kind of mum that my son deserved.

In my quest for this, I took Xavier to a music group at one of the local Children's centres which I thought he would enjoy as we always played music in the car and at home and he seemed to respond positively. As I took my seat in the circle I realised straight away that I didn't want to be there. There were too many older children running around, it was incredibly noisy and there was no control. Parents talked among themselves as their children ran amok and the organisers did nothing to change this. In actual fact they seemed oblivious.

As they started singing the songs it got worse. The woman sitting next to me was swearing down the phone at her partner during 'row, row the boat,' as her little boy came and took any instrument Xavier had off him. Then the partner that had been sworn at on the phone then turned up, stalked right through the middle of the music group and threw a letter at the girl before leaving. The other ladies, instead of being shocked like me, sympathised and started swapping 'crap men' stories. I actually found the experience a tad bit scary. A child came up to Xavier, yet again and snatched a maraca that my tiny baby was holding, then proceeded to try to hit him over the head with it. I looked around, horrified but if anyone noticed they pretended not to.

I was so taken aback that this happened at a baby group and I resolved not to go back again. Ever. The singing was pretty horrific too. I'm no Julie Andrews but still, it takes skill to make *BaBa Black Sheep* sound that bad. Although Xavier didn't seem to be traumatised by the experience, I certainly was.

I was talking to a friend about it and she said she had accidentally gone to the same group and had the same experience. I am not being overly critical (OK, yes I am), but it worried me that people seemed to think it was alright to swear in front of little children.

'I guess at least the mothers are taking them to music, that's got to be a good thing right?' I said to my friend.

'Yes but you'll find that many of them have been told to do so,' she replied. I felt sad then because Xavier might have lots of hurdles to jump but his mother would always be doing the best for him as should every mother, but it frightens me that that was not always the case.

As well as seeing Dr. P. all of a sudden we seemed to have more appointments to go to. One of the scariest was the heart specialist. Dr. P, wasn't unduly worried about Xavier's heart, because he seemed so healthy but because of the condition he had to be checked to make sure. I was told that it was unlikely Xavier had a heart problem because he wasn't a 'blue baby.' I was very glad to hear my child wasn't a Smurf.

I was terrified as I took Xavier to the hospital. He had to have an ECG and once again I tried to keep my wriggly baby still as they put those sticky things on him. It broke my heart a bit to see him wired up, especially as he fought against it and cried. Then we went and waited to see the consultant. She listened to his heart and then took him for a scan (no idea what it was called). I held my breath.

'There's a couple of small holes but then that can be normal in most babies under one. They usually close up in the first year.' Basically there was nothing immediate to worry about and Xavier was due back in a year, which was all good. Although part of me was sure that there would be nothing wrong with Xavier's heart I had still harboured a fear, as you would when it's your child.

Whilst at the hospital there was a woman holding a baby and she told me he had Down's Syndrome. She was very sweet in a lovely, sugary way; i.e not like me. Her baby was smaller than Xavier but four months older and had had heart surgery when he was just Xavier's age. He also needed a machine at night to help him breath. As I listened to her I realised I had no idea what to say. So I didn't really say anything. I smiled and nodded a lot.

'I really feel for you, and understand what you're going through,' she said to me. I was lost for words. I smiled but inwardly I wanted to tell her that she had no idea and more than that I had no idea what she was going through. Xavier hadn't had to have surgery, and he breathed on his own. Most nights he slept through. I'm not boasting here, not at all, but I didn't understand for one minute what this other woman was going through, it was far away from my situation; it was another country.

'But at least he is cuddly,' she continued. 'My older son hates cuddles so he, makes up for that.' I looked at her and again stayed silent; she must have thought I was a bit rude. I felt rude but was totally unable to behave differently. After all, what do you say?

Xavier and her baby had nothing in common apart from a diagnosis at this point in time. I couldn't understand her and she didn't really understand me. It did show me that my instincts were right, though, all children are different even if they share the same condition. It's just about time they are treated as such. And actually that should start with the parents.

I didn't expect this woman to be the same as me but she thought our children were the same immediately and that was what I had been trying to fight against, or what I was fighting against, or what I would always be fighting against. I think that was one of the first times I saw it. It certainly wouldn't be the last. What I wanted to say was that her baby was beautiful and brave and my baby was gorgeous and plucky also, but that they were as different as they should be. More differences than similarities.

Our experiences, including the fact that she had two children and a husband, were totally different.

Ages ago, when I first got the diagnosis, my friend from Australia phoned me and told me that she had a book for me.

'You might not be ready for it but I'm going to send it to you.'

'Right.' I was doubtful, and unsure, and I felt on edge.

'It's just I was in a charity shop and I went to the cook book section and saw this book, which was called *Expecting Adam,* and my friend Adam and I had just arranged to meet so I picked it up because of that but anyway it's about two Harvard professors that had a child with Down's Syndrome.'

'Right,' I took another breath. Still unsure how to feel.

'Look I just had to buy it, and I know you might not want to read it for a long time but if you do then you'll have it. It's beautifully written and the author is very smart and writes like you.'

We talked some more and I tried to be calm. I received the book and I read the back. Then I put it away. After the encounter at the hospital I picked it up again. Before I read it, I called my friend.

'Hi, I'm about to read the book. But you know this isn't my story, and it's not my experience and I am reading it as such.'

'You're right, it's not your story, Faith, but you might get something out of it.'

I did. It was a story that in so many ways was so alien to me that I couldn't identify with it. The only common factor, as at hospital, was the condition. There was nothing else in there. I was so grateful that I read that book, because it just reinforced something that I had been trying to shout about. We were not the same. Not in any way, shape or form, which is just how life is and how people are. It's just the way of the world and so Xavier is as different from everyone else as they are to him. And I am not, ever, going to let a condition get in the way of that.

There's no such thing as normal. I learnt that along the way. We were all normal in the way that no one actually is. My friends worry about their children constantly too; everyone wants them to meet milestones, to be healthy, to sleep through the night, to be bright and happy and wonderful. We might have different worries but worrying is worrying after all. And although my local friends have great husbands who are great fathers I have other friends where this is far from the case. I guess my

point is that we are all different as are our children and that is the way this world should work. Not by trying to get us to live up to a normal that simply doesn't exist. There is no such thing as normal which makes me feel normal after all.

Motherhood is a series of battles to be won, but it is never a war.

Twenty-Nine: Nobody puts my baby in a corner

Being a bestselling author and the best mum ever is a pretty busy existence. But you know life is often a juggling act. I see myself as having two jobs; two jobs I love. Of course there are never enough hours in the day, and I would like more, but we do what we can. Just recently I have been besieged by men who would like to date me; however I am so busy that I struggle to fit them in. But then perhaps I shall go to dinner with a few of them, after all a girl's got to eat.

This is what I really think about my son; if I didn't keep my expectations of Xavier high then I truly believe I would be failing him. Because if they are high, the worst that can happen is that he doesn't meet them, but if I kept them low the worst that can happen is that he does.

My life was slowly getting back on track, now I knew it would never follow the path that I imagined; I had readjusted and was choosing my new path. I still didn't believe that I had no control; I still believed I could make life work for me, for us, although it was nothing like my imaginings. I had been reunited with my fantasies; now I knew that my future wasn't mapped out there was still so much that was unknown. I was picking bits of myself up again along the way again, and I was losing weight, exercising and feeling healthier than I had in a long time, despite my weird diet. Which in the whole scheme of diets could be much weirder, surely? I wasn't eating baby food, (yes I had briefly considered it), and I wasn't only eating red food, now that would be properly bizarre. My diet felt a bit like the one diet. One meal and day and one bottle of wine a week. Those were my rations and I was doing quite well sticking to them. I told myself that when I had lost a bit more weight I would go back to eating a bit more like a sane person but that was some way off.

My problem is that I am not one of those annoying people who loves healthy food. I mean really? Those who would rather have a salad than a sandwich and a packet of crisps. Or fruit rather than chocolate. That just isn't normal is it? I love junk food, crisps are my proper weakness, salt and vinegar my absolute favourite, although I do like a variety. So dieting for me isn't easy because I have to give up everything I really love. Like Pizza and chips. And I didn't want to be one of those annoying people who said that the weight just fell off, despite them probably having a personal trainer, meals delivered and liposuction. Sorry, it was hard work so I just don't bloody buy that.

I had set the date for Xavier's Christening, having had tea with the local vicar, (terribly quaint). Xavier was going to be baptised in the same church my brother was Christened in, and where I used to go to Sunday school. I was pleased we had what felt like proper ties to the church and I had taken Xavier to the service there at times already. The older ladies loved cooing over him and Xavier lapped up the attention. See, he took after his mummy in quite a few ways actually.

I wanted Xavier's christening to be a huge celebration. I wanted to celebrate his life so far, and it was so important to me that everything had to be perfect. I even made the invitations myself because I couldn't find any I really liked. Honestly I was becoming a slightly dysfunctional and less good version of Martha Stewart.

I booked a local restaurant which overlooked the estuary to have lunch after the service and all that remained was what to wear.

There wasn't great shopping for either me or Xavier in my local town and I really wanted to look my best. So I went on the internet.

I ordered about five dresses which I had to pay for, and cost me a huge fortune but I had called the website and told them I would be returning some. I wouldn't know if I didn't try them right? My friend had had some input and initially I had about ten dresses which I had to narrow down. When they arrived I excitedly tried them on with the hat I had already decided to wear and my high heeled shoes. When everyone voted (it was like the X factor for dresses and my mum was definitely Simon Cowell), I had my dress picked out. It was a green MCQ (cheaper Akexander McQueen) and it looked great with my hat. I packaged and sent the other dresses back, although I did have to keep another one I'd grown a tiny bit fond of.

Xavier was harder. I decided that at five months he was too old for a Christening gown, which was really just personal opinion, but he looked more like a little boy now and I didn't want to compromise that or make him hate me when he was older and he saw the photos. I looked at christening outfits available to boys and on the whole they were pretty horrific. It all goes back to how dressing girls is so much easier. Honestly. However I did finally find him a Baby Dior outfit, blue silk trousers with straps and a matching cotton shirt with a silk collar. And it was in the sale. And it was his size. When it arrived I tried it on him and he looked adorable.

Those were my happy times, planning a party which was something I loved doing, and shopping. And I was expecting my family from Bath and five of my closest friends from London for the Christening.

And only one of them knew for absolute certainty about Xavier.

I believe that some people might still struggle to know how I could keep something this big, this important from people they profess to love. But it was simple really. For ages I had no idea how to react to the news so how could I expect anyone else to? They might have reacted better than me but I needed to be sure I knew how to cope before I was ready to open up. Although part of me still would never want to fully open up, I knew I had to.

I had been doing so well, but I had another meltdown, a relapse perhaps, and called J, Xavier's godmother to be.

'I have to tell people, I know that, but I feel like it's happening all over again.' She talked me through it and I now know that this might happen throughout my life. Events will bring everything back to the fore. Because often I forget about Xavier's condition when I remember or am reminded, I am floored by it. But that is how I have chosen to live our lives so I have to deal with it. And I will.

I think if I had told people in the early days when I was still unable to cope, the danger would have been that I would wallow in my own imposed pity. It kept threatening to get me, that was for sure.

I couldn't speak to everyone, the idea of a phone conversation where I might cry, and stumble over my words filled me with dread, and I needed to spell out exactly how I felt, so I used the medium I feel the most comfortable with; I used words. I knew that this had to be right, I had to get it just right. I sobbed as much as I did after the diagnosis as I wrote the letter. I sobbed as I sent it. But there was a relief as they all disappeared into the postbox; a weight that had been lifted. I had taken another step and although I had wobbled I hadn't fallen over. Not this time.

Dear…

It may seem a bit odd that I am writing to you but this is the best way I can express myself, and say all that I want and need to say. It might be a bit long, so please bear with me!

You may or may not know that Xavier has Down's Syndrome. It was diagnosed after the thyroid issue came up, so for the first few months of his life we had no idea, nor did the health professionals that surrounded him. Prior to the final diagnosis there was much debate, with the health visitors, the midwife, the surgery nurse and his GP saying that they were sure he didn't have it. Unfortunately they were all wrong.

The reason I haven't spoken about it until now is that there was a lot I had to process. I had to deal with the news in any way I could without falling apart, and to do that I needed to keep it inside. Please don't see it as an issue of trust or anything to do with our friendship; this was just what I had to do.

I have been through seasons of emotions. There was the disbelief that the gorgeous baby who had been perfectly 'normal', wasn't. There was my ignorance about the condition, with the pre-conceptions that I had about what it meant. I couldn't reconcile my beautiful little boy with the picture I had in my head of a ''Down's'' child. There was the feeling that I didn't want a baby with such a condition (although at no point did I not want Xavier). That I didn't want my child to have to go through life with such a disadvantage to start with. That I had failed somehow and been unable to produce a healthy, 'normal' child. That I was a single mother with a Down's baby.

Then there was the way I was told which was pretty terrible, and didn't give me any positive information. There was the internet which threw up articles that scared me even more, if that was possible, until I stopped reading them. My emotions were thrown into freefall. There was no control; that had all been taken away from me.

After I had sobbed until I could barely breathe, and held Xavier so tightly, as if that would make things better, I began to realise that what-ever happened, however I felt one thing was clear; I could do nothing to change the diagnosis. And once the initial shock (there will be shock which I will live with for the rest of my life), had faded I knew that whatever happened I had to find a way to cope. I retreated into myself, because I wanted to run away and the only place I could run to was my own head.

After seeing many doctors, health visitors etc, this is what I know about Xavier's condition. His diagnosis was late because it wasn't obvi-ous. It might have become more so and might continue to do so but at birth it wasn't and he doesn't have many of the physical characteristics. He breastfed without problems which they say babies like him can't, and as you know, so far his development is as any other baby; he has met his milestones and exceeded some. In all assessments he has had so far I am constantly being told how fabulously he is doing and how so far his physical development and his alertness is not an area of concern.

His lovely consultant, as you all know I have had problems with, is constantly surprised by him, is very pleased with him and that's my boy. He is doing great. He is putting on weight, he is doing all she should be, my baby might have a diagnosis that sets him apart from most people and will be there for his entire life but there is nothing wrong with him at the moment. This is why I refuse to use the word 'disabled' when I am talking about him.

I didn't realise but I was told there is big scale and Xavier is at one end, they call it 'minor'. But at the same time there is so much we don't know. We cannot know for sure how this will affect him exactly, the sweeping generalisations that they make about his condition don't apply to all children, again the breastfeeding is just one. I have since learnt that there are many others. Also, there are many health issues associated with it, his thyroid problem for example, but he has no problem with his heart, and his hearing is fine at the moment. Anything else we don't know yet because he is still so tiny. But what I do know is that every child has the right to be treated as an individual, because like any child they are. They might have a condition, they might have various limitations but 'they' are in no way all the same.

And that's what I had to remember most. He is a lovely little baby, who I love with all my heart. He's my Xavier, he's the boy that smiles and makes my heart beat faster, who cries and makes me feel sad, who wakes up in the night and makes me frustrated when he won't go back to sleep, who looks at me with such trust, such love that I feel so, so lucky to be the recipient of that look.

I decided when I could think straight again that whatever happens I don't want Xavier to be labeled. I know he will be, has already been but I will fight to give him the freedom to be who he wants to be. Because this shouldn't define a person; that is one thing I am sure of. Just as any 'disability' shouldn't. He is a lovely little baby with a condition. He is not a Down's Syndrome baby, but a baby who happens to have Down's Syndrome. I can't fix him, I can't take this away from him, although God knows I want to, but what I can do is let him be who he wants to be, needs to be and also treat him as normally as possible. When/if he has special needs I will address them but I refuse to anticipate them. We won't live our lives like that.

I also firmly believe that people respond to expectations. Therefore I refuse to lower my expectations of him. I take him swimming where he is already kicking his legs, moving his arms and making great progress; he *goes to normal baby groups where he flirts with the girl babies and their mums; he loves music and bizarrely the Power Rangers. He doesn't stay still, he turns himself over and holds his head up, he looks at everything around him. He is an amazing little boy who deserves the best. And that is what I can, and will give him. I shall continue to simulate, teach and nurture him in the way I would have done without the diagnosis. That is the only gift I can give him and that is the commitment I have made to him. I expect him to fight against the stereotype as he seems to be already because he is his mother's son and I can already tell he has inherited my fighting spirit.*

But he deserves love, unconditional love and he will always have that. I shan't let us be defined by this, I shan't feel sorry for him, and I don't want others to because he doesn't need pity and neither do I.

That said, I can't pretend that this is all fine. I am grieving for the life I thought I would have with my son, and having to adjust to a future full of uncertainty, potential problems and probable prejudice. I will have to accept that people might stare at him, make assumptions about him, and that will hurt me so much, but I have to remain strong for him, stronger than I have ever been. But at the same time I know that he will be fine because he is just such a magic little boy and in my heart I know that he was meant to be here and I was meant to be his mummy.

I am living with contradictions. I take pleasure in my son, but also fear so much for him. I know now I will always live with these contradictions. But I also have to remember that this isn't about me. It feels as if it is, but it isn't. It's about a gorgeous boy called Xavier who I know will bring sunshine into my life every single day.

I love you and hope that this letter will help you to understand why I was unable to talk about this sooner, and also how I still find it very hard to talk about. I am merely a new mother who is trying, desperately trying, to do her very best.

Loads of love xxxx

I'd said all I could say. I waited for the response. I wasn't unduly worried about it because the people I'd sent the letters to were my closest friends. It was more about the big step I had taken in writing and sending it.

Because as I said all along I didn't keep quiet because I didn't trust them or that I thought they would react in a way that would upset me. It was me that I hadn't been able to trust up to now. I needed to be clear enough in my head and I was. So now I could concentrate on throwing the best Christening ever.

When people replied it was pretty much as I expected. Everyone was supportive, one friend said that she was in awe of how relaxed I had been as a mother. They all offered me support should I need it. The ones that replied to me in writing sent emails that I will treasure.

On friend said; *I am thinking of you and sending you lots of love and hugs and kisses and wish I could be right there for you. I firmly believe your life will be all the better for Xavier in all ways, and you will deal with everything that happens, as you always do, with love and courage.*

Another said*: I don't feel pity for you or Xavier, I really don't. I know you are the best possible mother and you and he will have a wonderful life together. He'll be a confident child because you won't let him be otherwise and a charming young man. He'll be so loved how could he fail to thrive?*

I realised how lucky I was in many ways for the first time in ages.

There were a couple of incidents that didn't make me feel quite so lucky. One friend said to another that she didn't understand why I was keeping quiet about Xavier's condition because it was better to warn people. When my other friend told me this I felt incredibly angry. Xavier wasn't contagious and I didn't see the need to 'warn' anyone about him. That did hurt but I rationalised that this was something I would probably always have to deal with. I had taken a while to get to the place I was in and I was Xavier's mother. I tried not to expect too much from people, after all I hadn't been able to expect that much from myself when I found out.

Another friend and I actually had my only row. She basically was upset that I hadn't told her and it triggered words that actually, in hindsight proved an outlet for my anger. I told her that I needed to do what was best for my son and I needed her to understand I did what I was right for us. The row raged on a bit and she finished by saying that I couldn't expect her to be anyone but who she was. She was right, I conceded but I replied that she couldn't expect me to just accept her for who she was anymore. My baby came first.

We didn't fall out, we made it up and it was all forgotten. This was mine and Xavier's path, our journey, but other people were involved in that and I had to prepare myself for the fact I might not always like that. But apart from those two blips everyone was truly wonderful and a lot of my girlfriends shrugged it off as unimportant, and that was really all I could ask for.

It was getting slightly easier. The trail of people who saw Xavier, doctors, health visitors, etc, were getting a clear idea of my attitude. I wanted Xavier free from labels, judgments and preconceptions. I was aiming high; I know but remember I promised to get Xavier the stars. And I bloody well would.

Some shared my opinion naturally; others who didn't were starting to come round. I knew that it wasn't going to be easy, easier was pretty much as good as it gets, but there you go. I decided that motherhood is a fight for anyone in many ways, perhaps more so for some than others. But you never let anyone put your baby in a corner.

Motherhood is always putting your child first. It's as simple as that.

Thirty: Friendship and the country

Xavier's christening was a wonderful day. He looked gorgeous as did I. My friends and family were all there and it was just perfect. In the evening I went out with my closest friends, and it was so much fun. More fun than I had had in, goodness, I don't know how long. Whilst out with my friends, a gorgeous and very rich man approached me and although I told him clearly that I came with baggage, he said that it didn't matter because my hat was so fabulous and he asked me out to dinner.

The real world almost catches up with fantasy again, shocker. I had imagined Xavier's christening and I was determined that it would be the day of my dreams. Oh goodness, I am so selfish, of our dreams.

Although, let's be honest Xavier was five months old. He cared about eating and sleeping and smiling and not too much else. He liked watching television (bad mother lets her child get addicted to children's TV alert), and he sometimes played with toys but I was pretty sure he wasn't actually that concerned about his Christening. I told myself that when he was older he would look at the photos and be incredibly pleased that his mother had thrown him such a party but I wasn't sure that I really even believed that.

I believed that organising the Christening, something I had always wanted for him, was a step in the right direction. It was there with the other positive moves I was making, enrolling Xavier in swimming lessons, going out and actually making friends. But there was one more thing I had to do; I had to learn to drive.

My poor mum barely had her own life anymore. She was my housekeeper, my part time nanny and my driver. That was OK when I barely went out but now I was going to various different things, she was really tied down. Not that she complained, she didn't bless her, but I thought that whatever happened, wherever I ended up living I needed to be driving anyway. In my fantasy I would be able to afford a chauffeur, but that wasn't looking very likely at the moment. So I booked myself some refresher lessons and tried not to panic.

I was never the best driver. I finally passed my test after failing it five times and then the test guy only passed me because he was retiring and I was his last ever test. Actually that's probably not fair because I technically didn't do anything wrong, but he did say that despite passing me I could probably do with a few more lessons. I'd had thousands. And after passing my test I drove for a bit, but living in London I really didn't like it. I think part of it was that I had no sense of direction; once I was trying to get from North to South London, and I got stuck at Hyde Park Corner, I just couldn't find the right exit so I parked in a nearby NCP carpark and called someone to come and get me. It cost me a fortune. So I wasn't really cut out for driving and as pathetic as it might sound, I used to say some people were born to be driven. By that, I meant me.

So, it was about six or so years since I'd even got behind the wheel and I was worried that I would never be good enough to take my son around safely. I decided that I would only drive an automatic car; my mum's was one, because one less pedal and no gears had to be easier right? My driving instructor was lovely and she didn't even look scared. I think because I knew I needed to do this I really tried and also, driving in Devon was much easier than driving in London. It turned out to be far less scary than I thought and I turned out to be better at it than I thought. Apart from parking, but that's a whole other story. Soon I decided that it might be time to buy my own car.

I went to the showroom with my pram and I asked to see the smallest car I could fit it into. I tried it to make sure and the car was chosen on the basis of that. Oh and I said it had to be black. Someone asked me if I wanted a test drive but I didn't. Just my pram in the boot. It was just a little automatic car, and I didn't care about engines and stuff. Look how far I had come. I almost felt like a grown up.

So, I had made some decisions; I had made some progress. I loved organising parties and this was my first for my child. This was going to be a Christening, a celebration, not a pity party. No, pity, or sorrow was not on the guest list. My beautiful baby boy deserved celebrating, and I was going to do it with Champagne and in style.

Despite my best efforts promoting local B&Bs my friends from London managed to find North Devon's answer to Faulty Towers. A hotel in a very pleasant location, but with an interior that my interior designer friend found more than a bit offensive. I drove to the station along with my mum's friend to pick them up. It was slightly embarrassing as I allocated two of the girls to go with mum's friend and they both got in the back of his car as if he were a taxi. Apparently they entertained him on the journey home with their plans to buy land and buy a Bull to put on it in Cornwall (they didn't quite get that Devon and Cornwall were different places), oh and the bull would be called Bollard, and would make them a fortune, so I am sure he forgave them.

I met them all at the hotel, and as they checked in, immediately scaring the very scary looking manager, (who had a squeaky leg and a flatulence problem, I kid you not), I left them to it while I went home to change. I returned for dinner, and they showed me their interestingly decorated rooms. Honestly, it was as if someone had tried to put as many different styles together in one room as possible. I cannot even describe it; it was chintzy, and threadbare, floral with a touch of the Seventies. Part of me wanted to close my eyes and part of me wanted to slap a preservation order on the hotel immediately.

They had already made waves at their temporary home by the time I returned. T was feeling a little under the weather and she was cold and had got the staff running around looking for blankets, my friend who is an artist loved the hotel and ran around taking photos which seemed to unnerve the staff a bit. My friend's four year old son was bouncing around excitedly and it seemed that they had suddenly bought this unsmiling and quiet hotel to life. I am not sure the staff thanked us for it though.

The night before the Christening, we had dinner and I drank a little too much wine, but I was planning on having a fun weekend and it wasn't as if I was normally out having wild times. Actually about as far from it as you can get. And we weren't too wild, although from the looks we were getting from the other guests we might have been a bit. I am not going to apologise because I really think I deserved being allowed to let my straightened hair down. My friends asked the waiters to get the chef out so they could ask him about his potatoes. He was terrified, so much so that his trousers seemed to fall down with the shock of being confronted by my friends. I remembered then how things like this used to happen to us all the time.

We kept the hotel staff up quite late with our talking, and drinking and then I took a taxi home. It was a bit of a blur at the end. A lovely, warm, fuzzy blur though.

Xavier's Christening dawned and looked as if it might be a pretty nice day; it wasn't quite raining which was really the best I could hope for. With a slight hangover, I took Xavier over to the hotel for breakfast so he could see everyone before the big event. He had cuddles and saw his big 'brother,' and I had a fry up which wasn't quite in my only eating once a day diet, but I was having a day off.

I went home, and got dressed up and then we made our way to the church. I felt slightly nervous, although I am not sure why, but I so wanted everything to be perfect. Xavier was perfect, he looked gorgeous and I had scrubbed up quite well, if I do say so myself. My dress fitted anyway, which was a relief.

Everyone arrived and the service began. It was a quiet christening because it was outside the normal church service and it felt very personal. For a moment I felt a little unsettled as I stood by the vicar alone (well with Xavier). I though my single status was one of the reasons I wanted the service to be private. It was occasions when I felt glaringly like the odd single parent, normally there would be two proud parents standing at the font and I always felt guilty for Xavier about that. Anyway, I soon shrugged that off, and as the vicar anointed Xavier with water, he started to fall asleep. He then slept in the vicar's arms for the rest of the Christening. He slept on as I took him at the end, and as my brother tried to take photos, he stayed resolutely asleep.

We made our way to the restaurant, where we were greeted with Champagne before lunch. I really felt relaxed among family and close friends. As did my sleeping baby, clearly. I thanked everyone for coming, especially Xavier's three Godmothers. I know that it isn't traditional to have three Godmothers for a boy but to be honest there weren't too many male candidates in my life and the only two possibilities were atheists and didn't want to be seen to be hypocritical. So Xavier had three strong women to look out for him, besides me and my mother of course.

After a lovely afternoon, Xavier woke up, and he cried. Actually more accurately he howled. I think he woke up didn't quite know where he was, saw all the people who had come to see him and freaked out a bit. I calmed him down and then when everyone started to leave, my mum took him home so I could stay with my friends. We finished the wine in the restaurant (naturally) before heading back to the hotel.

One of my friends got it into her head that as she was in Devon (which apparently is in Cornwall) she wanted to play skittles. I phoned around and we discovered a social club in Appledore, a village not too far away, which had a skittle alley. We arrived still wearing our Christening outfits; hats, fascinators and heels. Everyone was playing bingo as we walked in and they stopped and stared at us. A bit like the scene from American Werewolf in London only we were posher. We carried on, marching to the bar and then the skittle alley. Despite my Devon heritage my friend was totally surprised to find I was rubbish at skittles. We then moved onto playing pool where we fared no better. After going back to the hotel for a nightcap, (I swear the manager was in his pajamas sleeping at the bar waiting for us to leave), I arrived home, some time in the early hours of the morning.

I am a terrible mother. I don't know what time I got home but when I woke in the morning, my mother had a very disturbed night with my child. I felt guilty and vowed not to have that much fun ever again.

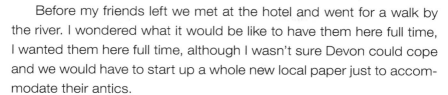

Before my friends left we met at the hotel and went for a walk by the river. I wondered what it would be like to have them here full time, I wanted them here full time, although I wasn't sure Devon could cope and we would have to start up a whole new local paper just to accommodate their antics.

I drove back to the station, and I felt like crying as I packed them onto the train with their Devon Cream tea that my lovely mum had made for them. They texted me to say they had drank the last of Great Western's champagne on the way back, and T had nearly been thrown off the train for trespassing in First Class, another friend had waded in ready to argue without any justification, and I missed them so, so much. They were going back to a life that I used to have too, but things had changed. Irrevocably. I think I knew then, more than anything that I would always miss them but I wasn't going back to London to live, not for the foreseeable future if not forever.

It was a memorable day and I felt a bit like I had fixed things a bit. Or fixed myself a bit anyway. I had overcome all the negativity to celebrate and that meant I was on the mend now, properly and truly.

Motherhood means accepting what you can't fix and fixing what you can.

Thirty-One: Step away from the child

People ask me all the time how I can be so good at being a mum and how come I make it look so easy. Well, I reply, if you read my bestselling book, 'How to be the best at being a Mum,' you will find all the answers. I am not a smug mother; I just work hard at being the perfect mum. And you can do it too. People say motherhood is hard, I say anything worth doing is hard, but the key to success is making it look easy.

No one said it was going to be easy. I can't remember reading anywhere that motherhood, parenthood, was a piece of cake. I didn't expect easy and I don't think anyone ever does. Not even people who fantasise as much as me. Don't get me wrong, it wasn't hard all the time. Sometimes it was actually easy and then you got lulled into a false sense of security, then bam it would get hard again. It's not that it wasn't worth the hard work, of course it was, but sometimes you just wished it could be a teensy bit easier. Who was I kidding; you often wished it could be easier.

And when you wished it could be easier you felt so guilty. You had the child; you loved that child, so how on earth could you moan about motherhood? It was a vicious circle of knowing that it was perfectly normal to feel like that, to wanting to keep quiet in case people thought you were a terrible mother. And the only reason you thought that people would think that was because you did. So back to the guilt again. I often felt like the worst mother ever even though I was far from it.

Here was my quick guide to motherhood. You were a mum when you feel tired at least ninety percent of the time. You spent the same amount of time, if not more, worrying. You felt like crying whenever your child cried. You found it hard to make a hair appointment. You had orange food marks on most of your clothes (although hopefully that stopped after weaning). You developed a crush on the tall guy from Cbeebies (and if you developed a crush on any of the animated characters then you had gone too far). You smelt your child's bottom despite vowing that you would never, ever do that. Actually you found yourself doing a lot of things you vowed you would never do. You wondered why you didn't have a full time nanny and if you would ever get a lie in again. Oh and of course you felt guilty most of the time.

The aftermath of the Christening was arduous for me. Every step I took seemed to lead to another crossroads and there were always more decisions to be made. And I was pretty crap at making decisions at the best of times. Even going out for dinner was taxing for me. I think I was just a bit flat too. My friends were safely back at home as were the rest of my family, and I was here, still here and I wasn't sure what next.

My baby was over five months old. I couldn't believe it had been five months since Xavier's birth at the same time as feeling that he had been with me forever. There was still so much I was going to learn about him, and learn with him and that was exciting. Incredibly exciting. But it was also scary. I didn't know what was round the corner; and I wasn't sure if I wanted to know or not.

There had been so many dark times and that had passed, really it had, but in its place was uncertainty. An uncertainty that I knew would be with us for the rest of our lives in a way, so I had to get used to it. I had to get used to a lot. But I realised that all parenthood is uncertainty.

I needed to balance being a mum with being myself and having my friends here had shown me that even more. I think that I knew how to be a mum, which is how it should be, but I was still a bit unsure how to be me. I would be lying if I said that I didn't feel a bit down about things because I did. There was still a lot to come to terms with and the pile seemed to be growing rather than shrinking. Being positive is the right thing to do. I have always tried my best to be a 'glass half full kind of girl', even when it seemed impossible to do so. I was doing my best.

Before Xavier, when I was still getting over my ex and trying to get my life back on track, I had tried to read those law of attraction kind of books, ever since I heard Noel Edmunds had made his comeback by following the Cosmic Ordering route. If it's good enough for Noel... I read a couple of them anyway, and I made lists, and I had a special box where I put notes and pictures of things I wanted in, and affirmation cards and all sorts. But I must have got it a bit wrong because what I thought I had ordered was a gorgeous husband, a big house, a successful career and children. Well I got the child but I was living with my mum and that was about that. Maybe I should unearth them again... Anyway, I was always trying to do the positive thing even when it felt as if I was swimming in treacle.

One the positive side, I was starting to establish good friendship here. There were some lovely mums at the groups I went to and at swimming lessons. Yes, they were all pretty conventional, in that they were either married or with partners but that didn't bother me so much. Well not all the time. Of course it got to me a bit, along with the fact that all the children were all 'normal', or condition-less, and that always made me feel a little sad. Not because I thought that there was anything wrong with Xavier. On the contrary he was such a brilliant little boy and there was no glaring difference between him and the other babies at this stage. But because I was worried about how he might have to struggle in the future. I wanted Xavier's life to be easy and although I tried to believe that it would, I also worried that it wouldn't. I worried a lot.

I think this was a big transitional period for me. Xavier would soon be six months old. I was still living with mum. He didn't have his own room, and I didn't have my own space. I was still feeling a bit teenage and yet I was a mother and a grown up and even a car owner. I had waved my friends back to London, knowing in my heart that I probably wouldn't be following them.

Although, as I said, I had already made decisions there were still a lot for me to make. I wasn't ready to make them. Yet I had to make them. Yet another basket of contradictions for me to play with.

But I had sort of decided that if not forever I was going to stay in Devon for quite a while. I went over in my head my options. Living in London felt wrong. I toyed with the idea of moving to Bath, another city I adored and where I had family but that felt wrong too. It came down to feeling safe again and although I didn't feel totally safe, I felt safest where I was. I needed my mum, I needed my brother and actually North Devon was a great place to bring a child up. I wasn't exactly unhappy there, and I would get used to internet shopping in time. Although I knew someone who lived in Devon who got addicted to the shopping channel and she bought all sorts of rubbish and her house was full of ornaments, so I really hoped that wouldn't happen to me. I couldn't guarantee it though.

In order to get used to the idea of staying in North Devon, I told some of my friends. A couple were pretty unimpressed and tried to argue that I needed to be with my best friends, (they had a point), but others seemed to think it was the right thing to do.

'You can learn to surf,' T, helpfully said.

'I can, and there will be loads of cute surfers around.' I was also in the process of convincing myself along with trying to convince them.

'Yes, you can go to the beach, find a divine looking surfer and then when he's not looking you could lie on his surfboard and when he asks you what you are doing you say "gosh, sorry, I thought it was my board". And when he points out that it's actually his, you say that you must have mislaid your board. Then he could help you search for it and when you never find it you can say it must have been stolen and then he will ask you out to dinner to cheer you up.'

'So, you're saying I should behave like a totally insane stalker woman.'

'Stalking, dating, it's all the same thing.' I loved T, but I resolved to try not to take her dating advice.

I was tired. All mothers are tired. There was nothing unusual about that. When Xavier was tiny I used to rest when he slept but now I couldn't really justify that. I would often be out while Xavier slept as well, either in my new car or with him in the pram. When my friend told her husband she was overtired he told her to sleep when the baby slept.

'What on the Link road?' she answered and I knew exactly how she felt. Not always but largely my lovely naps were a thing of the past.

Xavier and I were pretty busy now. We had lots of activities to go to, his social life was much fuller than mine, and also there were a few extra things thrown in because of Xavier's condition.

I resented every time a letter would arrive summoning my son to yet another check up for something or other. People might say that it was better that everything was being looked at and they might be right but I was feeling belligerent and I didn't need any more people to see. I didn't need more appointments, I hated my son being prodded and poked and wired up to machines. And my sunshine baby would often react to these appointments by objecting to them. He would cry and whine and rebel. It was as if we walked into wherever the appointment was he would know that it was somewhere he didn't want to be. You see, he was ever so clever.

I had to take Xavier for an eye test. I sat there in front of the woman, feeling pretty surly, perhaps even surlier than usual. I might even have been scowling.

'What are you looking for?' I asked as she waved some things in front of my five month old baby's eyes. Xavier squirmed on my lap and let out a little whine.

'Firstly to check he's not cross-eyed.'

'He's not cross-eyed.'

'We need to be sure.'

'I'd have noticed if my son was cross-eyed.'

'Not necessarily.' I resisted the urge to hit the woman, something that I seemed to feel regularly. But honestly, what mother wouldn't notice if their child was cross-eyed? It was ridiculous.

She then went on to say she was looking for early signs of short or long sightedness.

'What will you do if he is?'

'Well, nothing at the moment.'

I wanted to yell and pull my hair out. Or hers, I'm not sure which. I remembered back to the heart check, the other mother with the baby with Xavier's condition saying that they knew he would need glasses at some point. How useful was that to know? I wear bloody glasses and have done since I was eleven. Lots of people wear glasses. I didn't understand this and I really felt that she'd wasted my time. Which of course I didn't have enough of because no mother does.

But I kept quiet because I worried that if I didn't toe the line a bit they would send in social services or something. I was getting used to some people looking at me as if I was a little bit mad when I told them how I felt about Xavier's condition and how I was willing to fight it on my baby's behalf. I also knew that others totally supported my views and actively encouraged them. But I was aware that some did seem to think that I was in denial. Well I wasn't. Trust me I knew denial pretty damn well and I wasn't there. I had accepted the condition to the point that I knew it was there and I couldn't change it but I refused to anticipate problems that I may or may not have to face. If that made me mad then I didn't care because that was how I was going to continue regardless of what anyone said to me.

I knew then, instinctively that I would need to choose my battles. But at the same time I started to feel the burden of stress. I worried about the endless appointments which neither me nor my son enjoyed. I worried about how I would have the strength not to cry or shout as I went from one to another. I was under scrutiny, there was no two ways about it and people kept telling me crap that I had to fight against. I was more tired at this point than I had ever been and even when I slept I was plagued by worries. I guess that every parent of a five month old baby would say they were tired, there was nothing unusual in that.

However, most of all I worried that I wasn't being the best mother in the world.

I rushed to swimming one day, we were running late and I hate being late. Normally I am almost pathologically on time or early. I walked in, Xavier was in his carrier, and went to take my shoes off. It was only then that I noticed they were odd. They were both *Vans* but they were from two different pairs. One blue, one black. I was so embarrassed, I was mortified. I beat myself up about it. It worried me the whole lesson. I slipped them on as we were leaving and I pointed it out to my friend;

'I'm wearing odd shoes.' She giggled and looked at them.

'It kind of looks as if they are meant to be like that.' She then told me that once she had arrived at swimming without her swimming costume, and had had to borrow a horrible one that was too big for her that they kept there; a bit like at school if you forgot your gym kit they tortured you by making you wear the most horrific outfit they could find. So I felt better after hearing that. Of course I had to walk into town after swimming to meet my mother and I really felt as if everyone was looking at my odd shoes and wondering if I was trying to be cool.

That same week I arrived at a play date with my top on inside out; my friend very kindly pointed it out to me. Once again, I laughed it off but I felt as if I was losing the plot a bit. I left a trail of things everywhere. Baby massage I left Xavier's towel, another group I left his bottle, I left socks and all sorts of things all over Devon. I left things everywhere and I forgot things. I didn't leave Xavier on the bus but only because I didn't take the bus. The worst incident was when I went to a toddler group, pulled out the bottle to feed Xavier and realised it didn't have a teat in it, my bag was soaked as was my mobile phone and I had to rush home to feed my baby. I felt like crying, I was so inadequate, definitely not good enough to be a mum. Definitely not the perfect mum that my child deserved.

I felt as if I was losing it, but I wasn't really, because I was still mothering, just not perfectly, or as perfectly as I would have liked. I had, I admit, let things get to me. And by that I mean normal things. I was about to start weaning Xavier and that filled me with dread. I was the worst cook, and I wanted to do the best I could without really knowing much about it. That worried me. I worried about whether Xavier was taking enough milk because although he was putting on weight and everyone said he was fine, he wasn't the biggest baby still. I worried about our living arrangements because it was beginning to feel as if we were outgrowing my mother's house.

I worried about everything and anything. I worried about not knowing the future and I worried about what would happen if I did. Oh boy, I was

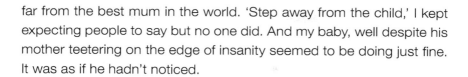

far from the best mum in the world. 'Step away from the child,' I kept expecting people to say but no one did. And my baby, well despite his mother teetering on the edge of insanity seemed to be doing just fine. It was as if he hadn't noticed.

Motherhood is letting go of being perfect, whilst striving for it at the same time.

Thirty-Two: Bless this Mum

I was happy with my life. I had a beautiful baby, a lovely home and car, and I a job that I loved and that was making me very successful and rich. What more could a woman want? Well, the love of a good man, of course. It wasn't necessary but it would be the cherry on the top of a very delicious cake. So, of course I wasn't terribly surprised when I met Mr. Right, a very handsome, successful man, who was incredibly funny and intelligent. He owned a bar and didn't like football. We hit it off straight away, in fact the sparks flew from the instant that we set eyes on each other. It was perfect and we fell absolutely in love. We became a family; one that wouldn't look out of place in a breakfast cereal commercial in fact.

Throughout my life when things were less than rosy I would always count my blessings. Sometimes I would write them down; other times I would play them in my head. I wasn't one of the people who managed to think that my life was fine because there were people in the world with far worse problems than me, oh no. In fact thinking like that threatened to send me into a depression. I hate suffering; my own and other people's. So instead I would count my blessings. When my father died there weren't many blessings but I did have my family, and my fiancé, a nice place to live, and a career. When my ex dumped me and I lost my home and my career hit the buffers I had a lovely family, fabulous friends and OK hair. You know the kind of thing.

Now, I had a beautiful boy, and no matter what condition he came with that was unquestionable. That was undoubtedly the biggest blessing ever. He bought me joy and I loved being a mum even when I thought I didn't. I had a wonderful family. I had amazing friends. I had my writing, something I loved and I was ready to go back to that. I had my health. I still managed to laugh. My hair was still there.

The first thing I had to do was to start weaning Xavier. One of my lovely friends had sent me a baby cookbook when Xavier was born and I poured over the pages, trying to understand what he could and couldn't eat. At first it seemed pretty easy. He ate baby rice initially and took to that wonderfully. It felt like a victory as some people seemed surprised that he ate off a spoon so easily. Then we moved onto pureed fruit and vegetables, (organic, naturally). That went well too, although he was partial to carrot and all my clothes had orange patches on them. I had these ice cube tray things that you put the food into, put it in the freezer and took out a cube at the time. It was genius so I could bulk puree and freeze. I don't know what I had been worried about. It was a breeze, and perhaps I was more of a domestic Goddess than I gave myself credit for.

This was a busy time and of course I still felt a little overwhelmed at times. I think all new mothers do. But now Xavier was six months, not only was he being weaned but our first visit to 'Brainwave,' the place I found on the internet, for Xavier to be assessed, was upon us. I was excited because this was my first positive move, but also apprehensive because some people were very negative about what they termed as 'early intervention.' I'm not going to go into this debate because it came down to me feeling that I was doing the best for my child, while taking that child, not just the condition into account. I knew Xavier was bright and alert and happy but I also suspected he was a tiny bit lazy. How had I reached this conclusion when he was only six months old? I just had. Call it mother's intuition. Or call me crazy. Either is fine. I didn't want to turn into a horrible pushy mother but I did feel, that perhaps it would be better if I pushed Xavier a bit, or encouraged as I preferred to think of it. I wasn't trying to turn him into some kind of genius, I just wanted to help him keep up with his peers where he could. And if he couldn't I wouldn't get upset but at least I would know that I had done all I could to help him.

We went to the centre which was only just over an hour away from where we lived. I felt nervous taking my baby there, like any parent you never really know if you are doing the right thing I guess. But when we had our first meeting I knew that it was the right thing for us. They asked questions about Xavier, ones which would give them the full picture of my child, questions no one else asked me. They didn't really make assumptions. They didn't tell me useless facts about my child's future. Which everyone else seemed to do.

There was no, 'his teeth probably won't grow in order,' (good to know), 'he might not know when to stop eating,' (maybe when I stop giving him food?), 'they are harder to discipline than normal children' (enough already). I won't go on because it's pretty depressing but I ignore it because I also think it's total crap. We go back to treating your child as an individual yet again.

After Xavier's evaluation, we saw on a chart that he was doing pretty well. Charts and babies are a bit rubbish to be honest as they are all different but what they did here was gave us the perfect child's chart and measured my child against that. Just so I knew what we were striving for. Not to upset me but to show me if there were any areas of grave concern. There wasn't at this stage and the reassurance I felt was priceless. Brainwave became from the outset one of the most important places for me and my son and would remain so.

Over the two days, Xavier was given a programme to help him. I was daunted because I was supposed to do this with him about four to five times a week and it would take at least half an hour. At first Xavier objected to it and I worried I would always have to make him do something he clearly didn't enjoy. I kept telling myself he would thank me in the end and actually after a couple of weeks he did seem happier as I put on our nursery rhymes and made a game out of our exercises.

I would be lying if I said this didn't concern me though. I was tired enough and trying to fit in just an extra half an hour a day wasn't easy. I fretted about it a lot. But we were determined and soon Xavier was thriving. I believed, rightly or wrongly that I really would be a terrible mother if I didn't do this for my child.

I remember being with family friends and me talking about what we did.

'You've got a pushy mother,' the friend said to Xavier. 'But you'll thank her for it one day.' I truly hoped that was the case.

My road was very bumpy. I decided that I needed to chose my next direction, it came back to the old chestnut of controlling what I could control, doing what I could to take us to the next step. There were two decisions I made. The first was that I would start writing again. Xavier was six months old and my maternity leave (not that I'd officially had any) was over. I would work for two days a week and mum would look after Xavier those two days. I knew, because of the nature of what I did that it would take me a while to get back into it properly but I needed to start, that was the crucial thing. The second decision was that it was time for me to move out of my mummy's house and get Xavier and I our very own home.

My decision to stay in North Devon seemed very real all of a sudden. I had no idea where I wanted to live, or how I would manage and it sent me into a panic. I also wasn't ready to give it my full commitment, just in case I really did want to go elsewhere, because I hadn't finally ruled that out. Someone suggested to me that I should look for somewhere in Braunton, a large village not far from the beach, which had a young vibe. Where my mother lives is gorgeous but the youngest vibe there is about seventy plus. Anyway, I went to check it out and I liked it. Of course I had been there when I was young but I hadn't been for ages. But there were shops and restaurants and pubs and if I lived there then I would be in walking distance of them (not sure the heels would hold up though). I could go and get a cappuccino in the morning without having to get in the car, and there was a choice of places to do so. I could go out to dinner if I ever had anyone to go out with. It wasn't quite London but it felt as if it was the nearest I would get in North Devon.

Unable or unwilling to make the full commitment, I started looking for rental properties. Ideally I wanted three bedrooms so mum could stay and babysit and just be there when I needed her. And also it would double up as a guest room if any of my friends ever managed to come back to Devon. I got the local paper and called letting agents.

'Are you looking to rent somewhere out or for somewhere to rent?' they asked me.

'Somewhere to rent.'

'Oh that's a shame.'

I wasn't deluged with choice. It seemed that Braunton was a popular village to live in. I thought about going smaller but then I realised we needed that extra room, otherwise my mother would have to drive back and forth if I ever went out and the living room would need a sofa bed and you know, I had compromised enough lately I didn't want to do it anymore. I felt a tad despondent. I assumed it would be easy, just as I always did and it wasn't. I looked in the paper one day and saw a private rental advertised. It was just what I was looking for on paper and I called up to make an appointment. I spoke to the lady and it turned out it was her daughter's house. And although her daughter had emigrated, when she lived in the house she was a single mother, and she had started out renting it and then been able to buy it. She lived there with her son and it seemed a little bit fated to be honest.

I knew other people wanted the house but when I went to see it I knew that it was just what I wanted. It was just what we needed. Set in a terrace, it was open plan downstairs with three bedrooms upstairs. It wasn't huge but it was perfect for us. Manageable. I set about selling myself and Xavier as the perfect tenants. I said I really wanted it and had to wait an agonising few hours before they called to say it was ours. Although I think deep down I knew that it would be our first home, maybe my law of attraction stuff had worked after all.

Despite it being a rental I was determined that our first house, our first home would be as perfect as it could be. I asked the landlords to paint it all white, as they were going to redecorate. I also asked them if they would pull up the carpets so I could sand and varnish the floors. They agreed. As it was unfurnished I started hunting in antique and second hand shops for furniture. I actually ended up painting everything because nothing I bought matched or was in very good condition. I bought chandeliers, and gorgeous light fittings, I pretty much changed everything I could without spending a fortune.

I really enjoyed shopping for our home, despite the fact that I was struggling with time. But I found gorgeous mirrors and picture frames and I had some Lloyd Loom furniture which I had re-upholstered. I was being pretty creative, because I didn't have an unlimited budget, but that was fabulous because it meant I felt my house was pretty unique. The only room I couldn't do anything with was the kitchen but hey, my kitchen requirements were still pretty basic. Somewhere to puree and store wine in fact.

When I first got the keys to the house I would put Xavier to bed at mum's and then drive over to Braunton to paint more furniture and organise things. I would then drive home, fall into bed and repeat the exercise the following day. I wanted this home, mine and Xavier's first home to be perfect for us before we moved in. I was pretty neurotic about it in actual fact.

I called a guy with a van to drive to London to pick all my things up from storage and I was also pretty excited to be reunited with my stuff. I had been living in and out of storage for years, since leaving for Singapore, and because the nature of moving around had lost things which still grated on me a bit. So it felt, for the first time in years that there was a sense of permanence about my life. Because all my things would be out of storage and I had a home which was just mine and my son's.

Sometimes, when I try not to feel like a victim, I do wonder if there is such a thing of bad luck after all. I never liked to think there was or that I was naturally unlucky because that is such a pain to be, but there are times when you really do have to wonder.

My man with a van's van broke down when he was due to go to my storage. I had to have everything picked up that day as we arranged that and so had to hire another van. He managed to get all my things back from storage but when he had to pick the rest of my furniture up his van still wasn't fixed. I had to pay to hire another van and ended up with three of the worst removal men ever. Rubbish removal men I called them. Two of them were still at school in all fairness, but they couldn't get my wardrobe into my room so they put it in the spare room. And they told me it would have to live there, because I had 'funny angles.' Not only did I not have the energy to argue (said wardrobe is still in the spare room), but I even tipped them. Goodness.

But we were nearly there. I had my furniture in and it was just about ready for us to properly move in and start living in our home. I got the blinds and curtains put up, and we were good to go. However at this exciting point, the electrics in the house started tripping and despite trying to figure out what it was I couldn't. I was painting furniture, by candle light, I was trying to get everything done, I was shopping which I loved but was spending a fortune on a house that I couldn't actually yet live in. I was exhausted. I hoped that I would never, ever have to move house again.

But at least Xavier's room was perfect. On his door was 'Xavier' bunting that I had had made for his Christening. And, when I was expecting him, Charlie found this vintage umbrella stand with soldiers around it. It was gorgeous and the theme for Xavier's room was decided before he entered the world. I had bought a set of gorgeous antique soldier pictures for his wall, found a Deco gentleman's wardrobe which was so perfect I was overjoyed with it. We painted his furniture white to match his cot and changing table, hung union jack bunting, and Xavier's room was ready for him.

The electrician said he had fixed the problem, which was great and we decided to move in. I was too excited. At half six, just as I was going to make Xavier's bottle for the night, the electricity went off again and in tears I loaded up the car and drove back to mum's. I sobbed myself to sleep that night and felt that somehow, yet again I was to blame.

Of course the electrician came back and did fix the problem and we moved in and had the first night in our new home. I felt incredibly emotional as I put Xavier to bed for the first time in his new room. Because that was what I wanted for him, a lovely home and a gorgeous room and although I was pretty sure he didn't appreciate it the way I did, he had and I felt as if I had achieved a lot. I had done a lot of it myself; I built Xavier's cot, I built my bed, I didn't need a man, I was a strong independent woman. Although technically I had used a few men to help, like the rubbish removal men, the electrician and a handyman for the things I simply couldn't do but I had managed to do more than I felt I was capable of. As I fell into my new bed for the first time I felt as if I had achieved a lot.

It might just be pureeing right now but I was even cooking for my child. I might still not have been the perfect mother but I was getting closer, to giving him what he deserved, surely I was.

If as a mother you ever need to count your blessings, then look at your child. They are the biggest blessing ever.

Thirty-Three: Loneliness – Part Two

Moving to my new home opened up a whole new world. Although Xavier had a pretty full social life mine still needed a bit of work. But, lo and behold I was immediately embraced by people in the village and I made friends immediately. I was deluged by invitations to parties and dinners and I really loved everyone. I was making friends, meeting cute men, and I really couldn't believe how life was so good. I was incredibly happy, busy and I didn't ever feel lonely.

It was inevitable I guess that one of the first lessons I learnt, living in my new home, was how incredibly spoilt I had been in my mum's house. Suddenly I had to do things, things that had seamlessly been done for me. Things I had shamelessly taken for granted like a little spoilt brat. I'm not even talking about anything major; just normal things. Like cooking my dinner. Cleaning. Shopping. Even making the bed. It was all a little bit of a shock, although my mother was still doing my laundry for me, which was at least something. I did realise, perhaps a little too late, how lucky I had been. Now I saw that if I thought there were not enough hours in the day before, there certainly weren't now.

One thing I learnt about motherhood is that there is never enough time. You always plan to get on top of things but you never do. Or at least I never do. I always have a mountain of paperwork to attack, letters to send, bills to pay, and so on and so on. I always said that I'd get everything organised when Xavier was in bed, and then after I'd put him to bed I would have my supper and then realise I had no energy to do anything else. Some evenings would be slightly more productive than others but nine times out of ten I would collapse on my sofa without the energy to attack what needed to be attacked and then the same would happen the next day. I needed a full time live in housekeeper, and then I realised I had just left one.

I might have missed my independence, living with mum, but not that much.

Domestics aside I was now awaiting my social life to take off (it hadn't even occurred to me that I didn't actually have the time or energy for one). I was ready to have a bit of a life for me now. Ready and waiting. Call me the eternal optimist but here I was in my new home and now all I had to do was wait for all my wonderful new friends to introduce themselves to me. But, it didn't happen. I thought that I would be inundated with invitations, but I was wrong. There were very few. Actually there were a couple and then there were none. I thought that no one liked me and that I had made a huge mistake, because this life might be best for my son but if his mum was lonely then it wasn't good for anyone. It was so incredibly horrible, and as much as I hated feeling sorry for myself I absolutely did.

I had many lonely moments since being pregnant and giving birth. I had left my social life, and my friends behind and I missed them both. I had a full day being a mummy, I had lovely friends who were also mums but in the evenings, once my gorgeous baby was happily snoring away, I was alone. And although I quite like my own company there was just a bit too much of it going on. Especially as now I had moved out of my mum's, I really only had myself to talk to. And it wasn't even that I got sick of my own company, it was more that I craved a tiny little social life. I wanted grown up company and I wanted to have a smidgen of fun. I wanted friends to chat to, even if they were only coming round to mine for dinner and a DVD. I wasn't asking for much, really all I wanted what I thought of as a bit of normality in my life.

I really loved going out. In London, before Xavier I spent most of my time out to the point where I would yearn for a night in, in front of the TV because it was a rare treat. I would go out for dinner, for cock-tails, to friend's houses, to the movies or the theatre. There was always something to do and somewhere to go and it was a lot of fun. Largely all single we had a bit of a party lifestyle. Don't get me wrong, I didn't want to go back to that. No, I was pretty tired most of the time so there was no way I could have done, but going out once a week would have been a start. Was that really too much to ask? But I felt as if now I was in my lovely home with my lovely son I had no where to go and no one to see. I felt isolated.

I wasn't totally friendless; my next door neighbours were lovely and we soon became firm friends. S, who was a teacher, and T, her doctor husband had recently returned from a year long trip to Canada, and S had lived in London until they married, so we had that in common. We also bonded over our love of shopping and antiques. They became two of the most important people in mine and Xavier's life almost im-mediately. So it wasn't that there wasn't anyone but for some reason I thought I was moving to a ready made social life, and actually I wasn't.

Of course I was being hugely naïve. What I was doing, when I moved to Devon while pregnant was starting over. I was leaving my old life behind, but of course then I thought I would be going back to it so I hadn't confronted that fact. But now I realised I was properly starting over again. I had moved to a new place with my child and that hadn't happened before ever.

I had moved from London to Singapore, but that was with my ex, so although I found that move quite difficult, I wasn't alone. I was living with him and I had ready made friends in the wives of his colleagues, some who I still keep in touch with and some who were so utterly frightening I often wondered if they were real. And goodness I wasn't alone now but if it wasn't for Xavier then I would have drowned in loneliness.

And since Primary school I had always found it easy to make friends. So the fact that suddenly now I didn't took me by surprise. I assumed that I would make friends wherever I went. My history had supported this, and I'm not boasting that I am incredibly popular but I certainly never found it hard, or worried about making friends. Perhaps people already had all the friends they needed, perhaps they didn't like me.

Oh goodness in my lonely state I really worried that perhaps I wasn't liked. But my mummy friends seemed to like me but, I still felt as if I had notched up yet another failure. I suddenly was able to add paranoia to my growing list of ailments. Poor Xavier, what had he got himself for a mummy?

It was, of course, more than just the fact I was alone. I did listen with envy sometimes when friends talked about their husbands, but not that severely. What I really envied was more that they had an extra pair of hands, someone to share in teatime, bath time, bed time, getting up time, paperwork and all the chores that I was really struggling with. I didn't immediately think of companionship, funnily enough, although in hindsight that would have probably been nice with the right guy. But, I didn't feel hard done by for being a single parent at all actually; I had always been this way, even when pregnant so I didn't really know different. I loved being with my boy and although I would have liked the conventional family, that was more for Xavier than for me. It was more to do that I had stepped out of my comfort zone; I had lost all my familiarity. Boy I was drowning in a sea of uncertainty and that resulted, inevitably, in feeling damn lonely.

Amidst all this life was busy and a little too stressful. I had Xavier's exercises, his swimming lessons, toddler groups, music, I had extra appointments, I was trying to work. I also was assigned a lady, a Portage worker, (I still don't really know what that means) to come to see us once a week. Although she was there to help and offer support I saw it as yet another thing that most mothers didn't have to content with. I was exhausted. I was sad and a little bit harassed. I yearned for a stress-free existence whilst knowing that I might never be able to have one.

The exercises were still hard. Xavier still didn't love doing them. I turned exercise into playtime. I put his nursery rhymes on, I used his favourite toys to coax him with and I tried to make it fun. He was sometimes happy to go along with it and at others he objected to them. Then I objected to it and we would both inevitably end up in tears. I felt guilty that I was making my son do something that he didn't want to do. Like anyone I guess, some days were good, others more of a battle. But I guess that is motherhood.

I was desperately trying to get Xavier to sit up and he wouldn't. Everyone talks about milestones. They are set out in a book I was given when I had Xavier which gives yet another chart that said babies should be doing certain things by certain times. It maps out everything from smiling to walking to talking. Of course all babies are different, but you get your chart and as a parent you want your baby to do what he should be doing within that chart. I felt this especially keenly. I didn't think that I should lower my expectations in this respect as in any other, hence Brainwave, and sitting was one of the first big things that babies do.

As difficult as it might be to admit, I cannot be totally sure of my motives at this time. Of course I wanted my boy to have the best start in life he possibly could. I was constantly being told that the older Down's Syndrome children got the further behind they fell. Well to me that was a red rag to a bull. I would feel so angry, and I don't know why. I was determined that Xavier was doing as well as he was possibly capable of doing and I didn't know what that was at this time, but I believed that if I could keep him as close to his peers as was possible now then I would always be able to. Therefore he would be able to go to mainstream school and not feel that he was too different. That was all I wanted for my child.

Also, I have admitted before to being belligerent and argumentative. No one tells me I can't do something, that just makes me more determined, well I was like that with my son. Part of me felt I had been made to listen to so much crap about my child that I wanted to prove them all wrong. Although a lot of the people who surrounded me now were totally understanding and supportive of my way of thinking, I still felt defensive towards them. You know, as much as I hate to admit it, at the time I think I wanted to prove the world wrong. And that started by getting my child to sit up.

Xavier didn't seem to be desperate to sit though, and although he hadn't missed the milestone (God forbid) or anything like that, I think I was using this to get him to prove me right, to prove that everything I had been saying was right and he was going to live a pretty good life. I put all my fears and hopes into my baby sitting up. Which I know is really bloody stupid, but at the time I didn't see that. I thought that if he sat, then he would crawl then he would walk and so on and there would be no glaring differences between him and his peers. I thought if only he could sit then life wouldn't be too hard for him, that he wouldn't feel that he couldn't do things simply because he could. I became a little obsessed and totally neurotic. I tried to hide this from my child, however, because he didn't need this anymore than I did.

I carried on with the Brainwave programme and we both began to object to it a bit less. I am not sure if the milestone chart becomes the bane of a parent's life or not, but I believe you can sometimes be a bit obsessed by it. I know lots of parents who are concerned about their babies hitting milestones, not just me, and the poor babies don't get a say in it. I think in my case, everything became enlarged. Amplified. Xavier wasn't the problem, however, I was.

And as I have said before each baby is different the way that us adults are. Some seem advanced, others a bit slower and boy there we all are with the bloody chart trying to ensure our babies are all the same. I think of it as the neurosis of parenthood.

On the positive side I was getting to know Xavier more and more as well. He was constantly developing in various little ways. As I said before, I thought he tended to be a bit on the lazy side. He had a play mat and in order to encourage him to move I would put the toys down on one side and put him on the other. Xavier would lift the play mat and try to drag the toys to him. Which I thought was incredibly clever, if not a little annoying. It was the same with sitting. We would do whatever we could to coax him to sit and he would topple over and I would get more and more despondent. One phrase people use with me is that Xavier will do things 'in his own time.' At the time I found that really annoying. I probably always will. But it's true for all children. They do all do things when they are ready but because of Xavier's condition we knew he was a little more flexible than he should be, and that he needed us to work on his strength. Although of course he would do it in his own time, I had to ensure I equipped him to be able to do so. It all came down to the fact that I felt instinctively he was capable, so therefore I wouldn't just let him do nothing, because I believed that if I did that he would do nothing.

In one of my more neurotic moments, I had a chat with my health visitor.

'What worries me is that I am going to push him too hard.' She looked at me and I looked at her. 'But actually if I do he'll tell me won't he?' She nodded her head. Yes, again everything came back to knowing my child and listening to him. It was just not as simple as it sounds sometimes.

I recognise that I am quite competitive. I don't really like losing and I'm probably not going to be the sort of mother who lets their child win at Monopoly, because actually I like to win. And if he does win then it will be because he is better than me and I shall sulk for hours. But I didn't want to be a super competitive mummy. I didn't want to compare my child because that is not for me to do. The swimming lessons we went to were great but I had to fight hard not to take them too seriously. At the end of each term we would get a report and if our child had done enough to pass, a certificate. Xavier started swimming at over four months old and that was late. Imagine these little dots being told to do better when they barely knew what was going on.

I actually found it funny, although I know some parents got really upset if their child didn't get a good report, or pass the term. I had to give myself a talking to. Xavier would kick his legs if he wanted to and blow bubbles if he wanted to. Goodness he would do whatever he wanted and I would support him in that. But you know with everything I was doing with Xavier, I had to reel myself in and remind myself constantly that this was about him, not about me and that was my constant chant.

On top of everything, my weaning was becoming less successful. I was trying to give Xavier lots of different food and he seemed to hate everything I gave him. Boy, motherhood was tough. I would spend all night (well until about eleven at night), chopping, steaming, pureeing and freezing food for him and when I presented it to him he would reject it. I was still filling the little ice cube trays still and I was having to remember to defrost food for the next day which sounds easy but when you were as tired as me, it's not. I was buying all organic, I was studying my Annabel Karmel cookbook because it said it was important to introduce your child to many different tastes and my son didn't seem to like anything I gave him. Yet again that best mother ever award seemed to be eluding me.

In my quest for domestic bliss, the only thing I wouldn't do was make my own stock. Please, what mother has time to do that? One day

I was given some organic baby food jars, that another mother didn't need anymore. I reluctantly opened one and fed my baby. He ate the whole thing. Who was this child? Drowning in guilt I bought more of the organic jars and although I persevered with my home cooking, my son definitely preferred the jars. I was betrayed by my very own child, in a way which to me felt as bad as King Lear! Well, perhaps not quite that bad. But I was very upset indeed.

But because I had always thought I was a bit of a hopeless cook, I did feel that my child was reinforcing this.

Remember how I said I always think of myself as a fighter? Well, this time I fought by trying to be that domesticated animal that I barely understood. Being new to the Terrace, I decided to throw an open house and invite the neighbours round. I was going to buy the food but no, instead, because lets face it I had oddles of time on my hands, I got my best friend to tell me how to bake cupcakes, then I baked said cupcakes and made cucumber sandwiches and everything. I would have even worn an apron had I actually owned one.

They came round and it was a lovely afternoon. The terrace I had moved to was a bit of a revelation. Only in one house in London had I become friends with the neighbours, in the last place I couldn't have even told you what they looked like. So here was a little bit of community and actually I really liked that. I might feel lonely on a bad day but I knew that there were people I could call on if I needed anything. So, there you go, another blessing to be had.

I was lonely and I felt as if I was coping but not much more. My son, the most important person in all this was thriving still. He was fed (even if it was from a jar), watered, and happy. Every activity we did he enjoyed otherwise I would have stopped it. He was beautiful, and he was loved. He was being encouraged, and maybe a bit pushed but that wasn't a bad thing. I know some people will criticise me for it but I knew, in my heart I was doing the best for him. But that didn't leave me with much energy for anything else. Let alone myself.

I found myself sitting at home in the evening drinking wine, (no not too much really, honestly, truly, OK maybe a bit). Comfort eating. My once a day diet was but a distant memory. No energy to go to the gym. My mum wasn't on hand to babysit whenever I wanted although if I asked her of course she would do it. I was gaining weight again. Maybe I was sitting in a type of depression but I don't want to exaggerate, it was if I was stuck in a tight space and I wasn't able to get myself out of it. However, I couldn't find motivation once my baby was in bed, I cried a lot now. I felt very lonely. I wanted to be in my house with my baby but boy I had really underestimated how terribly alone I would feel.

Neurosis is a part of motherhood. I defy anyone to say otherwise.

Thirty-Four:
Motherhood
without the child

Being an incredibly successful single mother means that at times I have to leave my son to go to very important meetings in London. I miss him like crazy but I also know that this is necessary to keep him in the manner to which he will become accustomed. And it gives me a chance to see my friends, to shop and when I get home I get the biggest smiles and hugs and I fall in love over and over again.

I've always liked the idea of meetings. I have no idea why because normally when you get the meetings they often disappoint. I had a job once (well a few actually) which meant a lot of meetings and what I remember most about them was that I struggled to stay awake and ate a lot of biscuits. As a writer meetings were actually much more fun and as you spent most of the time alone, just you and your laptop you welcomed them. But since having Xavier, meetings weren't actually part of my life and although I had started writing again, it was early days so no, there were no meetings. Unless you count Baby group and doctors appointments. I don't.

I left Xavier for the first time to go to London. It was a friend's birthday and I had planned a fleeting visit, well a weekend but it was the first weekend without my boy. Xavier was at home with my mother, so I didn't have to worry about him but I still did and I felt as if I had something missing. I had fun, but boy I felt puzzled, as if I'd forgotten something.

It was nice to go through the day not worrying about feeding times and naptimes and bathtime etc, what I mean was that it was actually lovely to have only myself to worry about for a change but of course I then felt guilty about that and then I worried about my baby. Would he be emotionally scared forever by the fact I left him when he was so young? I know it was only for weekend and he was with his Grandma but really how did I know he wouldn't always hold this against me? I guess you are always with your child even when you aren't.

I called my mum about one hundred times a day which must have been really annoying for her. Xavier was absolutely fine, and my mum and him had a lovely time too. Of course as he was only about seven months I don't think he missed me but boy did I miss him. I really enjoyed the break but I really looked forward to going home and seeing my bubba. And when he greeted me at the train station with a huge smile on his face I just melted. I hugged him so tight and didn't want to let go.

What was lovely for me, apart from the cocktails and shopping, (and there was a lot of both), was that I had a really good heart to heart with my best friends and despite feeling a little down they understood. I missed them, but was able to talk to them about everything and I wondered if perhaps it would be OK. Even if I had to go to London every now and then to be with friends, to have a social life then back to Devon for my life with my boy then that could work. I mean, of course it wasn't ideal but at least it reminded me that I wasn't alone; there were lots of people that I could turn to and I felt very lucky in that.

It was healthy for both of us, I was sure of that, and I justified that it was also good for Xavier because we were such a tight little unit that spending time without me, I hoped would be a positive thing for him as well. I knew I would do it again, other friends had left their babies and I wasn't the only one by far but again, mother's guilt lived with me along with the good times I had.

I believed mother's guilt kicks in especially when you felt you were being selfish. I understand now that as a mother you need time to yourself to be a good mother. It's simple but true. However, at the time,

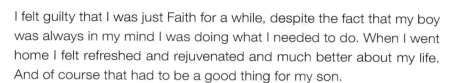

I felt guilty that I was just Faith for a while, despite the fact that my boy was always in my mind I was doing what I needed to do. When I went home I felt refreshed and rejuvenated and much better about my life. And of course that had to be a good thing for my son.

In my desperation to get Xavier to sit up I offered my brother fifty pounds if he could get him to do so. My brother took the bait and when I saw him after returning from London he greeted me excitedly.

'I got Xavier to sit up,' he said.

'I don't believe you, did you take pictures?' I am cynical and untrusting even with immediate family.

'Yes, of course.' He showed me the photos.

'I can see your hand holding him up.' My brother was foiled. Oh and that is why I am cynical and untrusting.

Xavier really liked watching television, I was sure that it was just the colours and sounds and movements that appealed to him (or he was a TV addict like his mother). When he was tiny and and I was feeding him late at night we would often watch 'Girls of the playboy mansion.' Don't call Social services, he wasn't aware at all and didn't even watch it as he was attached to my breast at the time but I really got into it. Got to love Hugh. But when he was bigger he would stare at the television if it was on, totally mesmerised, but more often than not it would be Cbeebies not E! His favourite programme was *'In The Night Garden.'* I couldn't understand it at all but Xavier would smile and get really excited and as it was on just before bedtime, I would give him tea, then his bath and then he would watch that before I took him to bed for his bedtime story and his milk. It became part of our bedtime routine.

One day he was watching it and I had to go and do something so I sat him on the play-mat, surrounded by cushions for the inevitable toppling. Only Xavier didn't topple. He sat up watching the entire programme and I was so shocked and excited I didn't know what to do. I called my mum and my brother and we were all thrilled. He was eight months old. He had made the milestone chart. It was a wonderful feeling for me. After that I knew he could sit but often he would still throw himself back which I'd previously taken to mean he couldn't sit. I learnt yet another thing about my son; if he wanted to do something he would do it. If it didn't, he quite simply wouldn't. I had a terrible feeling he was like his mother in this too.

When he was just over nine months he made his first attempt at crawling. He didn't get onto his hands and knees he embarked on what was called Commando crawling, as he looked like a baby marine as he dragged himself across the floor. But it was forward independent movement and that was another cause for celebration and Brainwave were delighted with him. I was delighted and he was delighted because he could now go and get whatever he wanted if he wanted. Once again I was a very proud mummy.

I took him on his first holiday to Scarborough in the summer. We were going to stay with one of my best friends and her family, the two girls and her husband. We had such a lovely time. I was relaxed, Xavier was divine. Adorable and very well behaved. Apart from the five hour train journey. Who thought it was a good idea to take a nine month old baby on that kind of train journey? Xavier didn't want to sit still, although in fairness other people in the coach were happy to entertain him and that helped a bit. As he'd recently started crawling he wanted to be down and have his freedom. Not possible at all. I survived but when my friend met me at the station I gave her my baby and asked for a stiff drink.

It was a bit of a revelation for me because I had the help of my friend and her two girls with my son and I really relished that. I suddenly wished I had an older child and wondered how she would feel about giving me one of hers. They helped with feeding, and bath time, they entertained Xavier and he loved the attention. I really knew that I would miss them when we left.

We went to the beach, and Xavier went in the sea again, which he loved although I found it a bit cold. I had taken Xavier into the sea in Devon of course and of course there were his swimming lessons. It seemed that whatever type of water he was presented with he would enjoy. I was pretty pleased, having decided to bring him up by the sea and really he loved the beach. He Commando crawled around at the beach and when he stood up he was covered, totally covered in sand!

He looked like a cute little sand monster. And as he laughed and shrieked with delight, I did too.

What was lovely was that we would spend the day with the kids, and then when Xavier was in bed I had my lovely friend to talk to and again, I didn't feel so lonely. Even distance couldn't obliterate that. Even the five hour train journey home with a wriggly baby who did not want to sit still couldn't obliterate that. Although, it nearly did.

Motherhood means that you feel guilty and selfish but that often means that you are still putting your child first.

Thirty-Five: Killing me with kindness

If I listened to certain people my son would be wearing special shoes, eating paint, and doing very little else. He might get a job when he's older, but he probably won't be able to take care of himself. His life expectancy would about 65 and he won't have children, probably, because there are only about 3 known cases of Down's Syndrome men having had children. My son isn't yet a year old and they tell me this.

What makes me angry is the threat that their 'realities' will destroy our reality. I can't have that. I still fantasise about the future, but I no longer imagine what Xavier will be when he grows up. Not because of the condition, but because although I don't really like surprises, we never know what our children will do, and that is the way it should be.

I think the pc term now is 'additional needs'; apparently Xavier will have some but we don't know what they will be or when they will appear. And as far as I am concerned, there are lots of children who need extra help in things, if it be maths, or tying their shoe laces or telling their left from their right. What I hate, and I am sorry but there has to be a bit of ranting here, is that my baby has been labeled 'special needs' before he actually has any. Go figure.

No parent knows what the future holds, Down's Syndrome shouldn't change that. I don't know what Xavier's additional needs will be, (although I accept he will have some). We don't know what his talents will be (although I'm sure there will be some). My role is to wait and see. To get him extra help if he's struggling with something; get him extra help if he is good at or loves something. That's how I see my role as Xavier's mummy.

Just as I won't go to the lone parents group I also won't go to the special needs group. It's like a private members club or something and I didn't sign up for a club and I won't join one. I am happy to hang out with other mothers but I choose the ones that I get on best with. I had spoken to Brainwave, to the Down's Syndrome Association and I had met other parents of children with Down's Syndrome. That was enough for me, for us, at this stage.

I worried that if I went to these groups I would be accepting the doom and gloom scenarios that I had first been given. I worried that I would be labelling and branding and stamping my child before he had had a chance to discover who he was. I didn't need the support of any other parents in my situation because I had all the support I wanted, and needed. You see Xavier didn't need a special needs group at this moment in time and therefore I certainly didn't either.

Yes, I did have the Portage service (must find out why it is called that). L, a lovely lady came round once a week and played with Xavier. Which was pretty great for me because it gave me a little bit of help and support and I could drink coffee while we entertained my son. She bought stuff for him, toys and playdoh, and they started to bond. I often wanted to kill her, and that was nothing personal; if George Clooney was Xavier's Portage worker I would have felt the same. Actually who am I kidding I wouldn't, I would have kidnapped him and made him stay with us forever, but that wasn't likely. I didn't resent her, I resented the need for her and I always will. She has come to understand the way I feel, she pretty much has always accepted it. She does say things about Down's Syndrome that annoy me but then everyone does. But it seems good for Xavier and therefore I am grateful for her. They have fun together, and she gives me ideas which I welcome. And of course she constantly tells me what a wonderful job I am doing with my son, which of course I love because just as my son really likes praise, his mother does too.

When Xavier learnt to clap he really loved it. He would have a big smile on his face as he clapped his hands together, looking very pleased with himself. I would clap back. I have always believed in praise as a way of parenting. Even when Xavier was tiny I would give him heaps of praise. I used it a lot when doing his Brainwave exercises as well. Hence the clapping I believed. One thing I loved about Xavier, was that when he thought he had done something clever, and no one acknowledged it, he clapped himself. Oh he really was his mother's son.

Still I resisted joining the special needs group. Not for a lack of invitations I might add. I was sold the group by one lady on the fact that there were two other mothers with Down's Syndrome children there. She told me this delightedly, as if I should be thrilled. I wasn't.

'To be honest that doesn't matter to me,' I said, and it didn't.

'We've also got a girl there whose had a tracheotomy.'

'Really?' What the hell else was I meant to say to that?

'She comes because its nice and quiet.'

'Oh, Xavier doesn't need quiet, he needs the opposite.' I actually believed this. What Xavier needed was noise and stimulation. My child was a noisy baby, often one of the loudest at baby groups. Quiet didn't really suit him.

But, anyway, she wasn't to be deterred. I swatted each of her arguments away but I will give her ten out of ten for persistence.

'This week we're making jam tarts,' she said in that very kind voice of hers. I imagined she was a bit of a head tilter.

'Xavier's seven months, he doesn't bake,' I replied dryly.

'No, I meant for you.'

There you go, being a mother of a 'special needs' child means you become so yourself. Although I do like a jam tart.

The truth is that just as my son doesn't have any glaring additional needs at the moment, and actually neither do I. Or perhaps I actually do but then I need to learn to deal with them. And that's the problem. Everyone is so nice, and so kind and I just sometimes want to punch them. (I never do I have never had a fight in my life, only imaginary ones).

I also know that people might think I am in the wrong, but I don't believe I am. Honestly, I have never been more right in my life.

I have to admit to always thinking I am right, however. With my ex we used to say the default was that I was always right and in the rare cases where I wasn't then I would perhaps admit it. And I wonder why my relationship broke up?

Anyway, I worried that if I only hung out with people in a similar situation to me I would fall into the special needs trap and I did believe it *could* be a trap. I've seen how people think that their children are going to be just as they are told, and you knew my feelings on that. No one can tell any parent more about how their child will be more than that child.

I accept that at some point Xavier might need to join the group, he will probably want to see other children with the same condition as him, in a way for him to accept it, which I think will be a good thing. And when he does I will be the first to sign up. I will suggest and encourage it when the time is right. But now, forget it. I intend on being led by my child.

Where I took Xavier to swimming lessons, which is just baby swimming, was in a special school (no idea of the pc term), because they had a hydropool which was much warmer for the babies. Once whilst waiting to go in with all the other mothers, and chatting, a lady (not there for swimming lessons), singled me out.

'How old is your little boy?' she asked.

'Nine months.'

'He's very young to be sitting.'

'Not really,' I replied, I was a bit surly, but I hated having attention drawn to me when I was in was with friends.

'Mine didn't sit until way after one.'

'Really.' I smiled but I couldn't have tried to deflect the conversation any more unless I had sworn at her. But although I can be cold and aloof I couldn't actually do that.

'Yes, he's twelve now.'

'We're here for swimming lessons,' I replied. I refused to engage in any more chat with her, and I fumed, silently as we went to the pool. I don't know why, I mean she was trying to be friendly but I just hate this comparison stuff as soon as someone thinks I am in the same club as them. I am sure her son is lovely but he's twelve and I could tell just by looking at her, and her manner that we had pretty much nothing in common. This happens to me a lot. Mothers with children who have the same condition as Xavier get excited when they see us. I don't. Do I feel like a bitch? Yes, constantly but I am, and that's it. I am not going to change and become a member of a club that I really never wanted to join in the first place. If a parent wanted to chat but not compare then I'd welcome that with open arms; so far none have.

You see, I did believe I needed support but the support I wanted was encouragement that Xavier was an individual, not a condition. That we were unsure what the future held simply as every parent was. That having a child with Down's Syndrome meant that I should react to his needs rather than pre-empt them. That as all people have different characteristics this was the same for those with Down's. No one told me this.

I talked a lot about losing your identity with the advent of motherhood. And I was still really trying to get mine back. It was somewhere out there, I was sure and little bits has been picked up a long the way but it also felt like a fight to get it. Even with a simple little thing like clothes. I didn't wear what I used to wear, not only because I couldn't fit into them but because my confidence had been knocked. I used to love wearing dresses all the time, but now I hid myself in the normal uniform of jeans and a top (which covered my muffin top and my hips and my thighs), gosh I was only one step away from a Burka, because I felt hidden I guess. And I knew, deep down that that wasn't me. But I wasn't sure who I was at that moment in time.

Just like I had never felt so unpopular in my life. I had never had problems making friends, I was even quite good at keeping some of them, but here I was, a girl I didn't really know. The mum part of me was OK. And of course I did have friends in the area and we didn't talk about our children ALL the time. But there was so much missing that I knew if I was going to be a good mother I needed to find myself. Just as a mother's job is to know her child, I also fully believe it is her job to know herself too.

About this time, having abandoned my child for a whole weekend I decided to see about getting him into a nursery. My mother was wonderful having Xavier twice a week but I saw a value in him spending time with children his own age and away from me. I wanted to foster independence in him, and confidence which I believe are precious gifts a parent can give to any child. You never want to think about them leaving you when they are tiny but you want to be sure that if they do they will cope. Part of me wanted Xavier tied to my apron strings (I still didn't actually own an apron but I really wanted one), but the sane part of me knew that if I could encourage independence in him then I would have done a good job. That wasn't just about his condition, and actually it wasn't just about me being a single mother. It was just what I had always wanted for my child even before he existed.

I knew immediately my nursery of choice. It was attached to a lovely Prep school that in theory I wanted Xavier to go to for his schooling.

I phoned up late one afternoon, when I had five minutes to spare.

'Hi, I wanted to enquire about the nursery.'

'Well there's no one there at the moment but I'm the Bursar so perhaps I can help.'

'I wanted to speak to someone because my son is nearly one and I wanted, in theory, to enrol him one day a week.'

'Great, it's a lovely nursery.'

'I need to tell you that he has Down's Syndrome.'

'Oh I wouldn't worry about that. We have two children in the nursery with Down's and you wouldn't know. Unless you looked really closely I guess. But they're no different from any of the other babies.'

I was sold there and then and made an appointment. Not because other children with Xavier's condition had gone there, but because it simply didn't matter to them. You see what I really wanted from life, and what I probably won't get is to keep Xavier from being labeled. It was probably hugely naive of me to think that any child could live that way. We all loved labels and we all loved to put people in boxes. Someone once told me that many parents are desperate to diagnose their children when they do anything out of the ordinary, for example ADHD. And for some labels offer huge comfort. That's the way it is. But I wish for my baby I could take that away, get everyone to treat Xavier as Xavier, but I fear that would never happen. But as his mother I could keep trying, and I damn well will.

Xavier had always attracted a lot of attention, even before the diagnosis. Once we were in a café with a friend and her baby and a woman marched up to me told me how beautiful my baby was and then put her arms out and demanded a cuddle with him. My friend was a little taken aback and I wondered if I should snatch my baby back or let this stranger hold him. I was within snatching back distance though!

I was always being told how gorgeous Xavier was and how cute and how wonderful. And he was. But I don't know if that attention is given for the right reasons. Don't get me wrong I have never had anything negative or nasty said about my child and I don't think I ever will, but I have had things which are in their positivity, negative.

One time I was walking down the street, pushing my baby in his pushchair and chattering away to him. A lady approached.

'He's lovely,' she said, bending down to smile at Xavier.

'He is,' I concurred.

'Children like him are special,' she added and I felt my blood boil.

'All children are special,' I retorted. If I could have a penny for every little compensatory sentence that had been flung at me I would be a rich woman with an even better shoe collection. I think if I have to listen to the bullshit then I bloody well should be paid for it. Bitter? Angry? Too right.

I was once told that I shouldn't worry because 'Down's children are usually good at music.' Yippee. Actually I did buy Xavier a guitar and he took pleasure in flinging it around the room, so there maybe he will be the next John Lennon. But, it's the 'They' factor yet again. 'They are so loving.' 'They are special.' 'They are so good natured.' They, they they. And I know that that is rubbish because each child is different. And I only had to look at my son to see that.

Yes, actually he really loved music (I do have high hopes for that). He was loving when he wanted to be but often pushed people away if they invaded his space. My mother would try to kiss him and he would take his little hand and push her face off of him. I actually found it quite amusing but she didn't. Anyway, he was his own person, he was not a 'they.' I would fight that forever. I fear I'll have to. I apologise for the rant; perhaps I should get myself a soap box and head down to Speakers corner with my megaphone and let rip.

I was also once told by a lady that her daughter went to the NCT thingy and there was a child there who had Downs' Syndrome but I shouldn't worry because he was invited to all the parties. She spoke to me as if I should be grateful. We were frequently with other children and other mothers. There was no exclusion and I don't think there ever will be. But I took it for granted; I wasn't grateful for it. I knew Xavier would be popular because he's such a charming, cool kid. Honestly, the fact that I was rubbish at violence was a very good thing I think. Imagine if I was like an *EastEnders* character I would be slapping my way around North Devon.

I was a pretty private person. Of course I have written this book which I hope more than one person will read so that might seem like a bit of a contradiction, but I've explained how long it took me to actually tell my closest friends about Xavier. Anyway, it was horrible for me to feel like I was such a public figure, that people could stop me in the street and so on. I would weep quietly when I was alone about that and I wished I could make them all go away. No wonder I thought about fleeing when I first got the news.

The worst incident for me was when I was sitting in the coffee shop with a friend and her little girl. A woman spotted Xavier and almost leaped over her table to get near us.

'Oh he's so gorgeous,' she shouted causing the cafe to look round. I felt myself colouring.

'You mean Xavier?' My friend asked. I was already dreading the next line.

'Yes. I've got one like him at home. She's eighteen.'

I have never been so offended in my life. 'One like him,' as if he was some kind of object; as if her daughter was. By someone portending to be being nice. The cafe looked away, I looked at my son. I turned away from the woman pointedly, too angry to speak. She hovered and eventually admitted defeat and went back to her seat. My friend looked a bit embarrassed but said nothing. We carried on having coffee but my day had been ruined. Why did people think my son was public property and that they have a right to comment on him? I shall never understand that and I hate it. I knew I was hugely over sensitive on this point but I also knew that wouldn't ever change.

Concerned more about the effect this will have on Xavier I discussed it with one of his Godmothers.

'I worry that he will hate the fact he attracts so much attention simply because of an extra bloody Chromosome. What is he going to think about this when he's older? What if he feels he's really singled out and although I am trying to teach him he is only who he is, these bloody people will make him feel different?'

'He'll be fine, he'll be so used to it he'll just take it in his stride. And I only think of him as Xavier, and so will anyone important to him,' she said. And she was right but I felt sad and angry that we would have to go through life in the spotlight and not in the way that we courted. I would rather people let us get on with our lives, let us be. I just want to be a mother and I want my child to be a child. Is that too much to ask? I really fear it is.

Not only do we have people trying hard to push us into a box, I also feel at times that I might be killed by some very misguided kindness.

Motherhood is not becoming your child, and not letting anyone assume your child is anyone but who they are.

Thirty-Six: I can't read maps

I am the perfect mum. I don my apron and I bake. I bake the most beautiful cake for my son's first birthday, I make the food. It is a huge success and everyone is in awe of the fact that I can do all this whilst coping on my own. I plan my next book, a book on throwing the perfect party for your child. Just as I am the perfect mother, Xavier, with his smiles, his laughs, his jokes and his love is the perfect child.

One of the things that people told me was that Down's Syndrome children teethed late. Well of course I took his information as I did every other bit I had been fed and I willed Xavier to grow his teeth. Just one would have done, just to show them that my son could grow teeth with the best of them. Anyway, as my friend's children's mouths filled up my son's remained resolutely empty. But from quite an early age we all thought he was teething because he would put everything in his mouth, clearly seemed in pain and he basically had the symptoms of teething.

I read somewhere that some babies didn't teeth until after twelve months, and that was unusual but still normal. But I also read that you should consult someone if your baby had no teeth by a year. So I would will Xavier to grow teeth whilst having absolutely no control over it.

'I'll just have to get him false ones,' I said to a friend. Only half joking.

One miraculous day when Xavier was eleven months on a tooth appeared. His bottom front tooth. Shortly after it was joined by another.

I rejoiced. My baby had two teeth before his first birthday and I was allowed to celebrate with Champagne. Utterly stupid I know but for me this was another victory of sorts.

Xavier's first birthday approached. I couldn't believe this little boy had been with me for only a year, yet I panicked that now he was a year old time was passing too quickly. I wanted my baby to stay a baby, yet he wasn't a baby he was becoming a little boy. A spirited little boy with a strong personality. A little boy with a smile that could light up a room, a temper which was pretty much like mine, which trust me is not necessarily a good thing. A charm that I believed would get him through life, and I wasn't sure if that was a good thing or not either.

A whole year and so many changes; the hardest year of my life; the best year of my life. We were booked in to have his one year check with the health visitor. Because I took Xavier to Brainwave, I didn't worry about these appointments, I knew exactly how my son was doing and I thought that that was probably one of the best gifts I got from going there. If it wasn't for them I would panic terribly. Would Xavier be doing the same without it? Who knows. Would I be? Definitely not.

I took him to our health visitor, who I really liked. She was always so encouraging, especially as she had known us for a year and had seen how we are getting on. The visit took an hour. Xavier had a few tests. She saw him sitting, she saw his commando crawl, she hid a toy under a blanket which he obligingly found and she got him to pick tiny things out of her hand. We got yet another chart. He was slightly behind physically, but nothing concerning. He was at his stage or above for everything else. He was at the fifteen to eighteen month old for comprehension. He was so clever. I didn't understand the tests really but I know that the health visitor who had always been a huge source of support for me was beaming with pride. We were all so proud of my son. But none prouder than me.

You might think this was just about keeping up with the Jones' babies, but it wasn't. It was to do with making sure that my baby has every advantage in life, and also letting him be himself within that framework. Sometimes I had no idea how to do that, but I would persevere.

Because that's motherhood. Sometimes you had no idea how on earth you are going to do it, what to do or when to do it but you keep doing it. You just do.

As my clever baby was about to turn one I wanted to throw him a party that he would remember. Yet again, remember the Christening? Not only would he not remember it but he probably wouldn't care. But I still wanted the best for him and I was determined to do it.

Key members of my family were coming, including Charlie from London, my local girlfriends and their babies. It was going to be a small party, but of course a little bit over the top. I hired caterers to cater. I did so because after all I still couldn't do too much more than boil an egg or purée. I didn't think that the adults would be impressed with that menu, so I ordered pies and quiches and salads and all sorts of nice things. Most of the babies would be able to eat sandwiches and bits I reasoned, but the food was mainly for the adults.

I found the number of a cake maker in a local magazine. I called her and arranged to go and see her. She told me she lived at the top of a very steep drive; unfortunately she didn't tell me not to drive up said drive. My car got stuck, one wheel was hanging off said steep drive, and when I tried to do anything the wheels just spun and went nowhere. I burst into tears and panicked because my baby was in the back and I felt as if I had put him in danger. We weren't in danger, though it was just pretty dumb. Although to this day I maintain that it was cake ladies fault. After all how on earth was I supposed to know that it was not a drive to be driven up? Anyway, I got out of the car, got Xavier out and the cake lady came down and surveyed the mess. I had visions of tow trucks and a huge bill but she called her neighbour and after half an hour of my pure panic, he dug up her drive and freed my car.

I was in such a state, as was her drive by the time we finished. I walked up to the house, she made me a coffee and I ordered a pretty expensive cake that we designed together. As my car was dented and scratched, it was probably the most expensive cake I would ever buy. I wondered if my little boy would appreciate it. I doubted that he would even eat it.

Charlie arrived the day before the party and hung bunting, and union jack paper chains that I had spent hours making. We opened the pre-birthday Champagne.

'Can you believe it's been a year since you did that mad dash from London?'

'No darling, it's mad isn't it?' I felt very emotional about my baby boy being a year old. When we finished decorating the house, it looked a bit like a royal celebration street party only inside and I had caved in; despite my aversion to balloons we had balloons. I had also made goody boxes for the babies, blue gingham with their names stuck on in felt letters. I mean honestly I should have written a book about how to host the perfect party. I was turning into the perfect mummy after all.

My little house looked lovely, Xavier was wearing a pinstripe jacket, a white Ralph Lauren shirt and a pair of jeans, he looked gorgeous. I wore a dress and heels and I didn't look too bad either. For me it was more than a first birthday, it was the feeling that we had made it through the really difficult period and come through the other side. I looked at my handsome son and I was determined, more than ever that this was just the beginning of a lifetime of celebrations. For us both, together.

Friends and family arrived and although there weren't that many of us, everyone there was important to us. Some of my friend's babies were older than Xavier, so some were walking, opening his presents and playing. Xavier was resolutely unimpressed with his party. He sat on the floor amidst his friends, and spent the first half of the party trying not to cry, then failing, and bawling his eyes out then finally he fell asleep. I put him to bed and I swear there was a look of relief on his face as he slept.

An eight year old boy had to blow out Xavier's candle because the guests wanted a slice of the mega expensive cake. Which by the way looked amazing, was delicious and turned out to be worth every penny. Well, maybe not the broken car. We cut the cake and we wrapped it and sorted out the good bags as my baby stayed asleep. He didn't actually wake up until everyone had left and of course we had to pose him by the cake as if he was blowing the candles out for the photos.

I wondered what Xavier would think when he was older and saw the results of his first two parties. Firstly, there would the lovely photos of his Christening and the video that was taken showing him mainly asleep. Then his first birthday party with the posed photos and the video showing him trying and then failing not to cry. What worried me most of all after the birthday party was that Xavier actually didn't like parties and never would. And of course I loved parties and always would and now I had a child I had even more excuses to have parties so where did that leave me? Almost hyperventilating at the idea, I decided that whatever happened, Xavier would grow to love parties. He just had to.

But again there is another thing I don't know about my child, and I will have to wait to find out. There is so much you don't know. Even at a year in there is a whole world of mystery ahead of us, ahead of both of us. That is what makes motherhood, parenthood so exciting and baffling at the same time.

My friends hadn't been to my house before and as they studied the photos on the wall they saw one of me as a baby with my father.

'Is that Xavier?' One of them asked. I looked at her.

'Have you seen the 70s wallpaper?' I replied.

'Oh yeah. My god, I can't believe how much like you Xavier is,' she said. They all agreed. They looked at Xavier and they didn't just see Down's syndrome. They saw me, they saw him, and so did I. For me that was a huge victory. One definitely worthy of another celebration.

For me, motherhood is a map, and I can't read maps.

Thirty-Seven: The future's bright

Sometimes you are forced to find the alternative to the perfect fantasy. But sometimes the alternative to the perfect fantasy is perfect in its own way.

Before Christmas I booked a week's holiday for Xavier, mum and I to Lanzarote. I thought some winter sun would do us good and also wanted Xavier's first holiday to be somewhere pretty easy for us. It was easy and we had a lovely time, however the hotel we had somehow selected was full of old-ish couples, mainly German, who went to breakfast and dinner every day and sat opposite each other not speaking and not smiling. I joked that that would be me one day. But in lieu of a husband that I could bore and who could bore me I would have to take Xavier with me. The poor boy would have no choice. And we would wear matching jumpers. I think my mother thought that she should probably take Xavier away from me right there, but I knew that it would never happen. If I ever ended up sitting across the table from someone who didn't make me smile there was no way it would be my son.

Oh and I promise I would never make him wear matching jumpers.

After Xavier's first birthday he started at the nursery that I had chosen for him. I think I was more terrified than he was, well of course I was because he didn't have a clue what was going on. The first time he went I left him and went downstairs for an hour and he didn't even notice my absence as he played contentedly. The second time the same. The third time I left him and had to go and pick him us as he was distressed. Yes, I did feel like the worst mother in the world that day. Then he slept nearly the whole time which, as you can glean from his birthday party is his coping mechanism (and funnily enough thinking about it, it's also mine). But after a lot of tears, both his and mine, he started to enjoy it. And then he started sleeping less, then he started eating well there and although he cried when I left him sometimes, I think that was to send me off with guilt, rather than because he was upset. When I returned to pick him up he always gave me the biggest smile ever and came over to me arms outstretched. And I was full of joy. Because I relished the day when I got to work but I also missed him terribly.

It was hard work. But I was determined to send him to nursery so he could learn a bit of independence and also if I am being honest, I thought it would be really good for him to spend time with his peers from a young age without me being there. I was his safety net and I always would be but we all needed to live without one at times. Of course I also needed to work so having him in nursery afforded me that but I also believed, fully that I did it for both of us.

Christmas approached again, and I did seriously worry that the nightmare of the previous year would cast its shadow over us. But it didn't. Xavier liked playing with wrapping paper, and of course was deluged with gifts; we were still opening them the following week. On Boxing Day I cooked a traditional Christmas lunch in my own house. I felt like such a grown up as I ordered the world's most expensive turkey (you see a pattern here with me and food), but apparently they did have very good lives, which was important and it came wrapped in tissue paper in a box. A very posh box.

I produced a proper lunch and felt very proud of myself. Of course I wanted to be a better cook because Xavier had slowly started eating some of my cooking and the older he got (and now he had a couple of teeth), the more variety of food we could try. He became a better eater and I became more relaxed about feeding him I guess. I think we both started to work it out a bit better. I got to know what he liked and used that as a basis to feed him. Anyway, it was a pretty jolly Christmas compared to last year. Although, that perhaps is not saying much.

In the run up I had been to a couple of parties and out for dinner with friends, so a social life was slowly calling me. I didn't cry that Christmas, I enjoyed being with my son which was just how it should have been last year but I was too busy to mourn that.

New Year's Eve life was very different too. Well for a start I wasn't waiting for a phone call. That phone call will be tattooed in my memory forever but it would never happen again. I thought I might feel that it was such a significant day for those reasons. I wondered if the year anniversary for the worst news I ever received in my life would hold a sad and mournful significance for me. Would I cry every New Year's Eve? I wondered if those horrible feelings would come up to the surface again. If I would feel the grief and the fear but I didn't. They were in my past. I didn't cry.

I wasn't as fearful of the future. I was actually looking forward to it. Don't get me wrong, I still bloody hate New Year and I didn't go out and celebrate, I was invited to go to a pub with some friends but I really didn't want to. I knew, now, that I had friends and would make more. I knew I had the best friends ever, even if they weren't down the road. I think perhaps I wanted to stay at home this New Year, to have some time to think, to look to the future, to embrace the future. But not to mourn, or weep or think of the past.

I did drink Champagne, that was a given, for me bubbles are appropriate at all times even if I wasn't in the midst of a huge celebration. Actually I often think that Champagne is better when one has nothing to celebrate really. But, actually, I kind of was having a huge celebration because when I looked back on the last year I had come so far. I never imagined I would even be able to come as far as I had done. Although of course I never imagined in a million years that I would have to.

I decided to make some New Year's resolutions. As with every year the first one was to lose weight. Boy, this time I really had to do it because at some point this year I would be running around after my toddler and I guessed being fit and slim would really help me in that. I also wanted to be able to wear my nice dresses again. Of course, I also resolved to nurture my son in the best way; to strive to be that best mum ever. I resolved to wear nice clothes all the time and look more like the old me. I resolved to find my identity, which I was slowly doing bit by bit. To wear make-up and my favourite red lipstick. I resolved to work harder and write this very story, the story that means more to me than anything I have ever written. I resolved to meet Mr. Right. I resolved not to push him away when I did meet him, (well some of my resolutions were a bit far fetched). I resolved, yet again, to be the best mother ever for my son.

I went to bed long before midnight that New Year's Eve, but instead of sobbing myself to sleep I just drifted into sleep. Even if there was still far to go, I had come such a long, long way.

I didn't know what the future holds, and I still had my fantasies, even if they were a bit watered down. Nothing was as I ever dreamt it would be, not ever. But it was. I am not saying this was a life I would choose; I wouldn't choose to be a single mum, I wouldn't choose for my son to have Downs' Syndrome or any kind of condition that makes life harder for him, but it's the life we were given. And we needed to make the best of it. It's not the life I wanted, or craved or dreamed of, but it is the life we got.

I still fantasise about the future. I would love to fall in love and if I'm honest I would love another child. I worry that Xavier and I are too small a family unit and I worried about what will happen to him if anything happens to me. But more than that I thought deep down that I always craved a family, and although Xavier and I were a family we are hardly typical. In a weird way we were the perfect family, at the same time as being pretty much the opposite. But we loved each other, that was a given and that would never be in question. Yes, I would love to meet someone and have another child and then be the family of my dreams. But you know, if it doesn't happen then I would still have a wonderful life with my son.

I was, however, thinking about Mr. Right having made the resolution to meet him. And when you thought about what kind of guy you want you can tread onto dangerous ground. I mean we all wanted rich, handsome, funny, and generous. Some friends said that when you got to my age you just want them to be single and a bit kind. Oh and if they had hair it's always a bonus.

But you know I had kissed my fair share of frogs so I deserved a prince. I wanted a man who was handsome, well-dressed, intelligent, who made me laugh, who made me smile when I thought of him. A man who filled my heart with joy. And then I realised I had him. I already had my Mr. Right.

But he was my son.

Because, you know, there were sounds that I loved, that made me smile irrationally. The sound of my new stilettos click clacking across the floor, a Ferrari engine revving up (long story for someone who is definitely not a petrol head), the sound of my own voice (no, really), and sometimes the sound of silence.

But there was one sound that surpasses anything I have ever heard, and that is my baby laughing. My goodness, I cannot tell you how happy that sound made me. Sometimes I would just look at Xavier and I would laugh and then he would laugh. At other times he would look at me and laugh and we would both laugh. It was the most heart-warming sound ever. Even if we had no idea what we were laughing at.

Xavier was really becoming the most joyous little boy, and I knew he had a bright future, I really did know that. Milestones, smilestones, he was really doing OK. I won't give up that fantasy, not for Down's Syndrome, not for anything. Call me crazy or deluded, I didn't care because I knew I wasn't, I knew that I was a mother, and I knew I was in love with my son.

It was full circle really; I was a mother. I happened to be a single mother. I also happened to have a child with Down's Syndrome. But first and foremost I was a mother, so whereas this was a story about me and my child, it was also a story about every mother and everybody's child

A mother can learn so much more from their child than they can ever teach them.

Epilogue

It's a warm but breezy Devon day. We are on the beach. I'm barefoot and the wind is ruffling my hair. I shiver but I'm not really cold. My little boy is running toward the sea, his laughter is caught in the wind and being carried back to me. His arms are flailing wildly with joy. The man is there. He is chasing Xavier. He is tall, he is handsome, he is kind and he is funny. He has some hair. He runs after Xavier until he catches him, and he throws him up in his arms and swings him around. Xavier shrieks with delight.

In my arms is a sleeping baby wrapped tightly in a blanket. Their face is pink and chubby and they snore, gently. He carries Xavier back to me; they are covered in sand but breathlessly happy. I am breathlessly happy. I kiss him and then pass the baby to him. I scoop up Xavier and give him a hug, trying to convey how much I love him, how proud I am of him. He smiles and me and I swipe a tear away. I never thought I could be this happy.

We look like the perfect family; we are the perfect family.

I will never lose my fantasies; they are still my best friends. And I will never stop searching for my Happily Ever After.

Printed in Great Britain
by Amazon.co.uk, Ltd.,
Marston Gate.